Pick Your Bottles

100 Wines to Change the Way You Drink

Dan Keeling

Quadrille

CONTENTS

Previous spread Condrieu, northern Rhône Valley

FOREWORD

Saturday night. 1979. Dad is still at the golf club but will be home soon. Sometimes it's a steak dinner on a Saturday night, with all the trimmings: chips, onion rings, fried mushrooms and the blistered skin of the halved tomato. The steak is always well-done. But tonight, Mum has made her lasagne. The pasta sheets, especially the ones towards the top, are brittle and glassy, splintering apart between your teeth. There will be wine for the grown-ups: the beaming sisters frolicking against the Alpine blue background of the Blue Nun label. Or the intricate, crenelated patterns – like the fossilised marks of tiny creatures in sea rocks – in the dark brown glass of the hulking bottle of Black Tower, standing menacing and thick-shouldered on the table. Or maybe something impossibly fancy like Hirondelle. An Italian white table wine masquerading under a French name. For supermarket customers it was safe, but with a hint of sophistication. At £1.39 a bottle in 1979, it had the right economic bouquet, though a Good Food Guide *survey that year rated it as no more than 'acceptable'. Mum will have dressed up and might be wearing her olive-green catsuit. Music, likely Sinatra, will be playing. My little sister will be toddling around, twirling her majorette baton. Me and Gary will be in front of the TV, where* Grandstand *will finally have given way to* Jim'll Fix It, *just before Dad gets home.*

– From *O Brother*, by John Niven

All apologies for the incredibly bad form of beginning a foreword to someone else's work by quoting from your own. But to properly understand how good and necessary this book is, you need to know – and be honest about – where you're coming from.

And I'm coming from the scene above. I grew up in a working-class household in the 1970s. It was a time and place where wine was a rarity and came in two forms: red and white. Then you go off to university, where you begin mixing with middle-class people and you start to pick up on certain little things. A 'dry' white wine is classier than the sweet ones you grew up with. (Much of this information is false – or misleading – but bear with me.) Older red wines, on the rare occasions you encounter them, should really be decanted. And it's pronounced 'REE-OKK-AH' not 'REE-OHH-JAH'.

Truly, a world of discovery unfolds before you.

Then it was on to the music industry, where I befriended my fellow record company A&R man and the author of this book, and where he showed admirable cunning in deciding Coldplay had a brighter commercial future than my peak signing of the time – Mogwai.

The bastard showed cunning in other areas too. While I spent a decade of expense-account dining learning just a little more about wine, Dan went deeper. I ended the 1990s knowing what Gewürztraminer was, and that I liked heavier Burgundies, and that I really wasn't wild about Sauvignon Blanc. But I persisted in making serious, expensive errors, like deciding I liked Pomerol, so why don't I just buy a whole, random case of the stuff without thinking about the producer or the year. Well, unsurprisingly, it turned out that you'd rather have a case of the clap than a case of that Pomerol. Meanwhile, Dan was learning how *not* to make those mistakes. He was learning about producers and vineyards and soil and years. He was learning that you don't take against an entire varietal because of a couple of bad bottles. He was learning that the ABV alone shouldn't be your entire guiding principle in choosing wine. What I really needed was a hand to hold mine. To tell me, "Okay, if this is what you're going to spend, this is what you want to be looking at."

Because, for most of us, buying wine is a little like I approached A&R, trying to find and sign successful artists, back in the day: throwing darts at a fucking board. And you don't really want to throw darts at a board, do you? You want to make a precise decision based on knowledge, budget and – most importantly – taste. It turns out that good taste – whether it's in music, food or wine – is an elusive quality. Indeed, there was an old saying in A&R that the ability to spot talent was almost as rare as talent itself. And here was Dan bloody Keeling doing with wine what he'd done in music: spotting platinum gems among all the dross. Facing down a wall of bottles in your local wine merchant is not unlike ploughing through a sack of unsolicited demo tapes back in the day. You're going to kiss an awful lot of frogs. What you don't want to do is marry the frog. (Like that case of Pomerol.) There was me, throwing darts at a board and scoring double one and a couple of sevens. Meanwhile, there was Dan – with his treble twenties, doubles and bull finishes. Man, it's enough to make you sick.

Thankfully, he's written this book. So now you can rock up and effortlessly throw 180 too. You too can look like a God of Wine to your friends, placing a fantastic bottle on the table with just enough of a spritz of information to make yourself sound clever without coming across like some awful wine guru.

We can leave that to Dan. Trust me, he's very good at it.

John Niven

START HERE

It's pouring with rain in Notting Hill, sometime in the mid-2000s. I duck into Lea & Sandeman on Kensington Church Street, its windows fogged, red buses grinding past outside. I'm looking for a bottle of wine that won't embarrass me in front of friends who know better. I've been coming in more often after work, but faced with shelves of names I can't pronounce, I might as well be guessing. "What do I bring to lunch for people who actually know Bordeaux?" I ask Stuart, a Scottish man who doesn't waste words. "Something that won't cost a week's wages." He scans the stacks, reaches down and pulls out a 2002 Château Larcis Ducasse as if it's the obvious answer. It's what he'd drink. That's enough for me. Because most of the time, I'm buying label art, prices, review cards – anything but the wine. That's the spirit of *Pick Your Bottles*: a friend suggesting distinctive bottles worth your time and saying, "Start here."

Whether you find yourself in a Manchester pub, a Siena *osteria* or a Lyonnais bar à vin, choosing wine you enjoy – and feel good paying for – takes practice. Keep tasting, pay attention and you will begin to know what you like long

Left Osteria Le Logge, Siena

Right Dan Keeling studying the wine list, La Cave des Voyageurs, Lyon

des Voyageurs
Bar à Vin

before you have the words for it. The wines that stay with you come from somewhere – not just a place, but a set of decisions. How the vines are farmed. When the grapes are picked. What the grower chooses to do, or not do, in the cellar. Open any of the bottles in this book and connections will start to form. A new music fan starts with Daft Punk and ends up at Nile Rodgers and Chic – same idea. In time, the names you couldn't pronounce become the ones you reach for first.

Pick Your Bottles isn't about the most exalted wines in the world – not many can afford them, and this book isn't written for the few who can. A single bottle of Romanée-Conti commands £15,000 or more (spoiler: that one's not in my cellar). Instead, I've focused on 100 wines I keep reaching for; bottles that drink far better than their price suggests. Most come from small producers with a clear point of view, not large estates working to a formula. They feel alive, not smoothed into predictability. I'll always risk the odd disappointment for the moment a wine makes me feel something visceral I wasn't expecting.

You don't need to read this book from start to finish, or in any particular order. Open it where you like. The 100 bottles are listed alphabetically by winery name. For each one, there's information about where it comes from and why it matters, together with notes on price, alcohol content and what to eat alongside it. All this is there to guide, not instruct. If something catches your eye, follow it. A grower you like tends to produce more than one good cuvée. A region begins to make sense. Before long, you'll start choosing differently, without quite knowing when it happened. You'll find familiar names sitting next to places you've never heard of. And every so often, without warning, a bottle will do more than satisfy – it will stay with you, and so will the grower behind it.

One of the most reliable ways to buy well is to start with entry-level bottles from leading vignerons. Dani Jiménez-Landi and Fernando García of Comando G make some of Spain's most compelling single-vineyard Garnachas, many of which sell for hundreds of pounds. Yet they also produce 'La Bruja de Rozas' at a fraction of the price – a lighter-bodied red that carries the same signature. Another approach is to lean on a sommelier's own enthusiasms. Ask what they've been enjoying lately when the service has wound down – especially at the bottom of the wine list, where value often hides. Or admit, without embarrassment, that you love Burgundy but rarely at its own prices, and see what they pour instead. Much of what's here is served at our Noble Rot restaurants, and I've included thoughts from some of our sommeliers on what they keep coming back to. When a carte des vins doesn't inspire, a Campari and soda is usually the best call.

As well as explaining why each wine in *Pick Your Bottles* matters, I also note whether it's farmed organically or biodynamically. Before the Second World War, every vineyard was organic by necessity; synthetic fertilisers and herbicides came in afterwards, when much of Europe was short of labourers. The best domaines today farm with greater care, often without formal certification. Walk through a chemically treated vineyard and the soil is dust, the rows are bare, you hear nothing. Walk through Jean-Marc Vincent's rows in Santenay (see p. 231) and the ground gives underfoot, the air smells of crushed herbs, the hedges are full of birdsong. Those grapes hold deeper flavour, the kind of life you can taste in a glass. The shortcut is everywhere on supermarket shelves: sugar added to boost alcohol, acid added to mask flatness, reverse osmosis to fix whatever was wrong in the first place – the vinous equivalent of a ready meal.

Good wine should be within reach. The heart of this book is in the £20–£35 range, with most bottles under £45 and a few set aside for special occasions. Whether you want an easy red for a Sunday lunch that rolls into the afternoon or a white worth lingering over at dinner, it's all here. If you love rosé, I'll take you beyond Whispering Angel to bottles with far more character. And you won't have to flinch when your garrulous pals knock them back without a second thought. This the book I wish I'd had when starting out: a friend's recommendations, full of discoveries and the occasional surprise, to help you pick better bottles.

Ten Characteristics of Great Wines

Jarvis Cocker speaks of a *tingle* – a physical response to music that feels instinctive, unmistakable. A shiver along the shoulders and down the back of the neck. When it happens, he knows he's encountered something special. I understand this completely. The same sensation exists in wine.

It isn't caused by perfection. In fact, perfection usually gets in the way. The tingle comes from vitality – from something alive in the glass. And, like music, wine does not act alone. It needs a listener. A drinker. Your mood, the day you've had, the place you're standing – all enter the equation. The wine meets your consciousness, and if you're both receptive, something happens.

People like to speak of mystery – that X-factor cliché – and there is truth in that. But mystery does not mean randomness. Over time, you notice patterns. The wines that give this sensation have harmony without rigidity, character without exaggeration. They carry the imprint of a place and of a person who respected that place. They have tension, energy, layers, nuance – a sense of movement rather than polish.

The tingle is fleeting, and you cannot command it. You can only increase the odds by paying attention and seeking out bottles that share certain traits. What follows is an attempt to describe some of the qualities I've noticed, over time, in wines that are likely to offer that sensation:

- They are crafted by people who care, their intent evident in every detail.
- They are cared for at every stage, from bottling through transport and storage to service.
- They speak clearly of origin – not just grape varieties, but where they come from.
- They possess a voice so individual you could recognise it blind.
- They offer intensity of aroma and flavour without excess, without the heft of wines pushed beyond what the fruit can bear.
- They are harmonious, with no element – acidity, fruit, tannin, alcohol or oak – drawing unnecessary attention to itself.
- They hold your attention for the entire glass, not just the initial impression.
- They deepen as you drink them, leaving a persistent, resonant finish.
- They age with grace, gaining nuance rather than simply accumulating years.
- They satisfy both the palate and the mind – pleasure first, but never without substance.

NB: These qualities don't guarantee the tingle. They simply create the conditions in which it might appear – and, in the end, that's all you can hope for.

HOW TO BUY WINE

Value Isn't the Same as Price

Wine has become more expensive, as everything has. But the idea that 'serious' wine only begins when the price starts to hurt is a myth, pushed by those who mistake expense for meaning. What has changed most is not the ceiling, but the floor. Even modest bottles are now consistently ripe and made with a level of care once reserved for grand estates, and offered without fuss as wines meant simply to be drunk. Buying well today has less to do with spending more, and more with knowing what to look for.

Buy the Least Expensive Wine Made by the Best Grower You Can Find

The person who makes the wine matters more than the appellation, the vintage, the grape variety, or any medal or score. A good *vigneron* almost never makes bad wine; a careless one can make very expensive wine.

Don't limit yourself to the specific bottles mentioned here. Once you trust a producer, you can usually trust their range. In moments of decision – standing in a shop, scanning a list – confidence is worth more than novelty. So it makes sense to choose the wine of a conscientious grower over that of a mediocre one, even if it costs a little more. That does not mean climbing a producer's hierarchy. Often, their entry-level cuvée is not only the cheapest but also designed for the moment in which you'll actually drink it.

When You Drink Matters as Much as What You Drink

Enjoying wine is about context. The same bottle can be perfect one night and out of place the next. Don't open a magisterial Montrachet for an aperitif with friends you haven't seen in months, when its subtleties will be lost in conversation. Serve something delicious, rewarding but undemanding, like a Domaine de la Pépière Muscadet 'Briords' – and if you have a short story about why it matters, so much the better.

A lightly chilled Beaujolais Villages suits dinner in the garden on a warm evening, when a powerful Barolo would feel out of place. That same Barolo, with a veal chop in November, comes into its own. There is no such thing as the 'best' bottle in the abstract – only the right one, at the right time.

What You're Really Paying For

One of the anxieties people bring to wine is not knowing what they're paying for. The difference between a £25 bottle and a £150 one can be vast – but not always in the ways the price tag suggests. Sometimes you're paying for land and history, sometimes for time and labour, and sometimes simply for rarity: the pleasure of drinking something that barely exists.

At the lower end of that scale, grapes often come from larger vineyards, farmed efficiently, with higher yields that keep the wine affordable. At the upper end, they tend to come from tiny, obsessively worked parcels in prized

terroirs, where labour is done by hand, yields are kept low, and selection is so severe that a good deal of fruit never sees the inside of a bottle. None of this guarantees greatness – but it does explain why two wines can look similar on the shelf and feel worlds apart in the glass.

Cheaper wines are usually made to be drunk on release. They reward immediacy. More expensive wines, by contrast, are often built for the long haul – layered, structured and capable of revealing new dimensions over time. They ask for patience. Both can move you.

When Buying for Later Is a Different Business

It's estimated that around 90 per cent of wine is consumed within a week of being bought. For most people, the idea of owning a wine cellar belongs somewhere between a vintage Ferrari and an estate in Provence: lovely to imagine but unlikely to materialise. In the UK, though, many wine lovers do something far less romantic but just as practical: they buy wine and leave it resting in bonded warehouses until the day it's withdrawn and drunk.

That His Majesty's Revenue and Customs allows wine to sleep this way – without duty or VAT until delivery – is a quirk of British trading history with few equivalents. It makes buying wine this way not just sensible, but often cheaper in the long run.

Still, buying wine to drink ten years from now is a very different business from buying it for next week. The former rewards faith and patience; the latter should be guided by freshness, drinkability and pleasure in the moment. There is an irony here: some of the world's most celebrated cuvées never make it out of bonded vaults at all, endlessly traded, never fulfilling their destiny – to be opened and enjoyed.

Where You Buy Matters

Where you buy your wine matters more than most people realise. Supermarkets source bottles that meet tight specifications – consistent, familiar, inexpensive – but those constraints demand volume and uniformity. The result is wine engineered to behave, often with the help of additives and heavy processing, stripped of the texture and individuality that make wine feel alive.

Independent merchants work under different conditions. Build a relationship with a good one and you gain more than access to bottles: context, conversation, discovery. Ask questions. Listen. Look out for the bargains – brilliant but awkward producers, wines priced long ago and overlooked. Pay attention to how merchants communicate what they're excited about. Wine-Searcher is a powerful tool for tracking down specific bottles online.

In restaurants, make friends with the sommelier. Ask what they drink when they're off duty, when no one's watching and no one's paying the bill. You'll learn more from that answer than from anything printed on the page.

Learn by Paying Attention

When I first started paying attention to wine, I saved the labels from bottles I loved, pasting them into a scrapbook alongside who I drank them with and what we ate. These days, I'm more likely to photograph a bottle and post it to Instagram. The method matters less than the habit. Over time, you begin to notice whose tastes align with your own – whether through friends, merchants or review sites such as CellarTracker – and discovery becomes less about scores than shared sensibility.

Photographing bottles is a good way of remembering what you like to drink. What a label tells you depends on where the wine comes from. In France, for instance, grape varieties are often absent, the emphasis falling instead on place. Vintage matters, though not always in the way it's presented. Some of the most extraordinary wines I've drunk were made in years dismissed as difficult. A thoughtful grower can coax beauty out of tough conditions, and while those wines may lack the density of so-called great vintages, they often offer something else in return: openness, clarity and a willingness to be enjoyed sooner.

When a critic says, "Drink date: 2029–2040", remember this is an educated guess based on how similar wines have behaved in the past. Wine is not governed by deadlines, and it rarely behaves exactly as predicted. I've drunk plenty of bottles long past their supposed moment that were said to be finished years earlier and yet were very much alive.

No One Knows Everything – and No One Ever Could

Buying wine well isn't about never getting it wrong. It's about getting it right often enough, and enjoying the process. No one knows everything about wine, and there's no need to try. A small corner, well understood, will do. If you have the space, buying a case of a wine you enjoy is one of the great pleasures of drinking. Open a bottle now, another in a year or two, and notice how it changes. Over time, the wine teaches you more than any tasting note could. Occasionally, if you've bought wisely, the numbers may work in your favour. But that's incidental. Confidence, in the end, comes from repetition. Accept the disappointments, return to the bottles that gave you pleasure, and trust your preferences to evolve.

FOLLOW THE IMPORTER

Why the Name on the Back Matters

There aren't many upsides to Britain being outside the EU, but one bureaucratic quirk works in the curious wine drinker's favour. Since 2024, UK importers have been required to display their names and addresses on wine labels – a rule long established in the United States, where importers' details must appear on every bottle. Why does that matter? Because once you notice importers' names, you realise they are the real tastemakers: the palates behind the wines you already love. If you've fallen for the charms of Provence's Domaine Tempier Bandol, spotting the same importer's mark – "Selected by Kermit Lynch" – on an unfamiliar bottle is a good sign you might enjoy it. In other words, follow the importers you admire, much as music lovers follow record labels, and you'll find the next big thing before the rest of the world catches up.

I've had two careers I've loved – as an A&R man at Parlophone and Island Records, and now as a wine importer – and the same obsession with discovery runs through both. Britain has talent scouts who've built stellar wine companies, their logos enough to make me want to taste something new: Nick Brookes at Vine Trail; Zubair Mohamed at Raeburn Fine Wines; and Eric Narioo and Doug Wregg at Les Caves de Pyrene. Across the Atlantic, Kermit Lynch; Grand Cru Selections; Louis/Dressner Selections; and Thatcher's Wine share that same instinct: taste you can trust.

Left Kermit Lynch, Berkeley wine importer

100 WINES TO CHANGE THE WAY YOU DRINK

Key

●○○○○	£10–£20 Better than it should be.
●●○○○	£21–£35 Where some of the smartest buying happens.
●●●○○	£36–£55 Wines that hold the dinner table.
●●●●○	£56–£100 For serious eating.
●●●●●	£100+ Wines that define the landscape.

The following 100 bottles are arranged alphabetically within five retail price bands, marked on a one-to-five scale. Most cost less than £45, with the heart of the selection between £20 and £35. A handful of rare and expensive wines appear as reference points – not trophies, not status symbols, just markers on the map. You don't drink them every day, but it helps to know they exist.

Every wine comes with a food recommendation.

1

Domaine Andrée 'L'Envolée'
Notes on a Neglected Grape

Region
Loire Valley, France

Grapes
Grolleau Noir, Grolleau Gris

Price
●●●○○

ABV
12.5%

Food
Pâté de campagne with cornichons; roast chicken with thyme, garlic and lemon; roasted beetroot with herbs and yoghurt.

There are grapes that history has overlooked – not for lack of character, but because no one ever thought to pay them enough attention. Grolleau is one of them. Before encountering 'L'Envolée', I too dismissed Grolleau as a rustic Loire Valley table-wine grape – relegated to industrial rosé and grown for volume rather than expression. What Stéphane Erissé at Domaine Andrée so compellingly demonstrates is that Grolleau's reputation has more to do with yield than any inherent limitation, revealing a grape capable of producing a light-bodied red of real beauty, perfectly attuned to how many of us like to drink today.

Erissé came to wine the long way around. After starting out as a builder, he changed course, spending several years apprenticing with Antoine Foucault at Domaine du Collier. Foucault is the son of the late Charly Foucault of Clos Rougeard – a domaine that, for many, set the bar for Cabernet Franc in the Loire. When Erissé struck out on his own, he purchased just 3ha in Saint-Georges-sur-Layon, much of it planted to Grolleau – a contrarian choice. The vineyards sit on schist, a soil capable of giving formidable tannin, so he opts for the gentlest extraction. The result is a wine of remarkable lightness and depth, with a perfume of violets and forest undergrowth, carried by a spicy, mineral edge. 'L'Envolée' – 'the Flight' – is something of a manifesto: proof that Grolleau, treated with restraint, can indeed soar.

2

Domaine des Ardoisières 'Argile Blanc'
Wines with the Safety Rail Removed

Region
Savoie, France

Grapes
Chardonnay, Jacquère, Mondeuse Blanche

Price
●●●○○

ABV
11.5%

Food
Best alongside simple Alpine fare – freshwater fish and mild mountain cheeses, such as Tomme de Savoie or Abondance.

Way up in the steep, slate-strewn slopes of Savoie – terrain that looks like it actively resents human involvement – you'll find Domaine des Ardoisières. This is not polite wine; it comes from harsh Alpine vineyards where everything has to fight to survive, yet somehow what emerges is defined by a striking crystalline clarity. The whites taste like cold stone, melting snow and thin mountain air. Wines scraped straight off the rock face, unfiltered, unapologetic and not remotely interested in making you comfortable. Which is exactly the point.

Domaine des Ardoisières lies in the shadow of the Château de Miolans, a ruined fortress and former prison whose most infamous inmate was the Marquis de Sade. It's a brooding yet fitting setting, capturing both the austerity and colourful history of this remote corner of south-eastern France. Not so long ago, a 'good' vintage here was one that the locals joked they could clean their windows with without it eating into the glass. Today, thanks to Domaine des Ardoisières, among a handful of others, those days are over.

One of my favourite cuvées in the cellar, 'Argile Blanc' brings together Chardonnay and Jacquère in equal measure, with a smaller share of Mondeuse Blanche. Though Chardonnay is hardly native, winemaker Brice Omont uses it here in service of the region's native varieties, framing rather than obscuring the Alpine character of Savoie. The fruit comes from vines that cling to the friable slopes above Saint-Pierre-de-Soucy – a village between Chambéry and Albertville, where the Alps seem to rise directly out of the vineyards themselves. 'Argile Blanc' is tense and flinty, wired with a line of acidity that snaps you awake like cold water to the face. For adventurous Burgundy lovers willing to stray off the beaten track, 'Argile Blanc' offers something both recognisable and thrilling.

3

Bodegas y Viñedos Artuke 'Artuke'
How Little Do You Really Need to Spend?

Region
Rioja, Spain

Grapes
Tempranillo, Viura

Price
●○○○○

ABV
13.5%

Food
An easy-going red built for weeknight meals, this goes well with everything from sausages and lentils to *pasta al pomodoro*.

Right Arturo de Miguel Blanco of Bodegas y Viñedos Artuke

Next spread Artuke's Finca de los Locos vineyard, Rioja Alavesa

Once in a while, a friend sidles up asking for a number. What's the minimum, they ask, that they should spend for a decent bottle of wine? Having become desensitised to the inflation of recent years by close proximity, the question makes me reconsider everything I think I know (of course that over-performing Mâconnais has quadrupled, stupid). So instead of a figure – because no price guarantees that a winemaker has good taste – I remember recent bottles that far surpassed expectations without making me blush at the cost. And it hits me all over again that many of them come from unfashionable places like Rioja, where, once you've circumnavigated the oceans of dross that have devalued their standing, you'll find a galaxy of undervalued wines like 'Artuke'.

Rioja blossomed in the late 19th century, when *bodegas* began supplying a French market whose vineyards had been destroyed by phylloxera. Inspired by Bordeaux, they enjoyed decades of success producing long-lived reds and whites. But industrial farming and widespread modernisation in the 1980s and '90s led to a decline in individuality and quality. Reluctant to abandon a proven formula, many *bodegas* set out to create wines with more power, colour and alcohol – and, in their minds, greater prestige – but instead made lakes of lifeless vino that few drinkers want today. So much so that some vineyards have even been left unharvested in recent years.

Rioja has never had a worse reputation. And yet, somehow, it's never had more small producers doing things the right way. Through responsible farming, low yields and judicious handling of the grapes in the winery, Artuke's superb 'La Condenada' – along with the top cuvées of growers such as José Gil and Carlos Sánchez – stands as an antidote to homogenisation. But when it comes to the 'what's my number?' question, it's Artuke's humble *tinto* that really gives me pause. A foot-trodden Tempranillo with a splash of white Viura, made using carbonic maceration in a supple, Beaujolais-like style, it makes me wonder whether this might be the least anyone could spend in this book and drink well. How does Artuke do it? It doesn't matter. Just be grateful it does.

PJL 1973 Club
PEPE JEANS LONDON

4-5

ASSYRTIKO
No Delicate Flower

Hatzidakis 'Familia'

Region
Santorini, Greece

Grape
Assyrtiko

Price
●●●○○

ABV
14%

Lyrarakis 'Vóila'

Region
Crete, Greece

Grape
Assyrtiko

Price
●○○○○

ABV
13%

Food
Assyrtiko is good with *kleftiko* – a slow-roasted leg or shoulder marinated with garlic, lemon and oregano, sealed in foil, and cooked until tender.

When the locals of Santorini drink Assyrtiko alongside slow-roasted lamb, you start to understand that this white is no delicate flower. It's a powerful, salt-licked survivor that takes on red meat as if settling old scores. Almost everything about it is uncompromising. It thrives in volcanic soils where nothing else grows. It gets blasted every summer by the Meltemi winds, the kind that peel paint from fishing boats, yet survives through an ingenious system of basket vines known as *kouloura*. And despite Santorini's vineyards having shrunk to a quarter of their size over the past century, sacrificed to the island's tourist industry, the grape refuses to fade away. Perhaps the biggest challenge the island's wines now face is whether drinkers will accept the steep price rises of recent vintages, driven by a tenfold increase in grape prices paid by winemakers to growers in the last ten years.

Haridimos Hatzidakis was the grandmaster of Santorini Assyrtiko. He pioneered its first organic vineyards and crafted whites with bold, unyielding personalities. His tragic passing in 2017 was a profound loss to anyone who valued the artisanal honesty of his wines, set against the output of the island's commercial wineries. Today, the Hatzidakis family carries his legacy forward, producing cuvées that show the grape at its most uncompromising. Assyrtiko needs good ripeness and sufficient alcohol levels to shine, and Hatzidakis does not shy away from either. Broad and bone-dry, 'Familia' delivers its hallmark salty-lemon-mineral edge, drawn from vines up to 80 years old that are tended by the family's cousins, aunts and uncles.

For a taste of Assyrtiko without paying the Santorini premium, eastern Crete's Lyrarakis 'Vóila' cuvée is hard to beat. While it doesn't have quite the same crackle as Santorini, it shows that crisp, saline citrus edge that defines the grape. Textured and pure, it has a way of exceeding expectations.

6

Franck Balthazar Côtes du Rhône
The Back Door to the Northern Rhône

Region
Rhône Valley, France

Grapes
Syrah, Grenache

Price
●○○○○

ABV
14%

Food
Perfect with a bowl of lentils, lamb on the grill, garlicky sausages, or anything cooked over fire.

The growers behind some of the Northern Rhône's most sought-after wines – Côte-Rôtie, Hermitage and Cornas – also make Côtes du Rhône that are a pleasure to drink and cost very little. A few years ago, the Côte-Rôtie *vigneron* Jean-Paul Jamet poured a mysterious red, without saying what it was. One of my friends, an eminent Rhône wine expert, called it the 1985 Côte-Brune, his top wine. When it was revealed as his 'simple' 1998 Côtes du Rhône, we sat there, as baffled as dogs at a magic trick. Likewise, for all Franck Balthazar's fame for Cornas, the wine many drinkers covet most is his modestly priced Côtes du Rhône – a lush, dark-toned red from organic old vines around Séguret.

Balthazar is the nephew of the late Noël Verset, one of the masters of Cornas, and he carries on that legacy. His cellar is small, his production tiny – just a few thousand bottles a year – but every one of them speaks of the old ways: whole-bunch fermentation, native yeasts, restrained sulphur, and a devotion to the vineyard that borders on reverence. If you come across a bottle of his Côtes du Rhône – or, if you're lucky, his Cornas – don't hesitate to buy it. His Côtes du Rhône is often on Noble Rot's by-the-glass list, where it manages the rare trick of pleasing both the uninitiated and the hardened Northern Rhône purist. The Côtes du Rhône appellation itself is vast – a patchwork of soils and slopes stretching across the south of France – and often its name is attached to forgettable cooperative wines. But in the hands of a grower like Balthazar, Côtes du Rhône is honest wine, made as it should be.

7-8

BAIRRADA
Where Portugal Crackles and Fizzes

Quinta das Bágeiras Garrafeira Tinto

Region
Bairrada, Portugal

Grape
Baga

Price
●●●○○

ABV
14–15%

Filipa Pato & William Wouters 'Nossa Calcário' Branco

Region
Bairrada, Portugal

Grape
Bical

Price
●●○○○

ABV
12–13.5%

Food
In Bairrada, suckling pig borders on religion – as persuasive with Baga as with the region's sparkling wines – while shellfish sharpens the line of the whites.

Left Mário Sérgio Alves Nuno of Quinta das Bágeiras

Next spread Mugasa, Sangalhos

When my pal the Spanish wine critic Luis Gutiérrez tells me there's a place in Bairrada, central Portugal, turning out the finest suckling pig he's ever tasted, I don't reach for a guidebook – I reach for my coat. He is a man not prone to hyperbole. And when he mentions, almost as an afterthought, that a *vigneron* in that same town of Sangalhos poured him a more than 30-year-old sparkling blend of native grapes that redefined what Portugal is capable of, I know I'll soon be knocking on both doors.

Mugasa is one of those restaurants that does not need to advertise. In Bairrada, it barely needs a sign. People drive two hours north from Lisbon just for the suckling pig – its blistered skin giving way to flesh so tender it scarcely holds its shape; no theatrics required. Mário Sérgio Alves Nuno of Quinta das Bágeiras eats here as many as ten times a month. You would not guess it. With a glass of his 1991 Espumante Velha Reserva alongside – its burnished oxidative layers and peach-skin freshness slicing through the richness – it comes close to perfection. Yet, as so often happens, you arrive for the headline act and leave thinking about the supporting cast – other grapes, other wines.

Bairrada, an appellation blessed with good limestone soils between Porto and Lisbon, sits close enough to the Atlantic to feel its cooling breath – a gift in a country where heat is seldom scarce. For decades the region was shaped by the belief, still common in Portugal, that good wine required scale, with many farmers selling fruit to cooperatives and larger houses. That orthodoxy is loosening. A generation of small growers now bottle under their own names, turning out incisive sparkling and still white wines from Bical, Maria Gomes and Cercial, alongside age-worthy reds from Baga – a grape with bright acidity and stern tannins that, given time, resolve into perfume and poise.

Alves Nuno, alongside fellow veterans such as Luís Pato, was among the first in modern Bairrada to champion quality-focused, estate-bottled wines that had long been sold in bulk. His Garrafeira Tinto is a brooding, old-vine Baga: full-bodied and structured, with leathery savouriness and firm, chewy tannins that demand patience. It sometimes

RANGLER
Sport
Jeep

Left Filipa Pato, Bairrada

evokes a hypothetical seaboard Nebbiolo and will appeal to traditional Barolo drinkers – particularly when made in this old-school fashion, with whole bunches, native yeasts and large oak barrels. In an age obsessed with restraint, it's a red that remembers what shoulders are for – and is none the worse for it.

Just down the road in Óis do Bairro, Filipa Pato and her sommelier husband, William Wouters, tend their limestone like Burgundians marooned on the Atlantic. 'Nossa Calcário' – 'our limestone' in Portuguese – is Bical stripped to its bones: no make-up, just the kind of nervy white wine that makes that fashionable tasting-room descriptor, 'salty', feel less like metaphor than truth. Filipa is the daughter of Luís Pato, who helped safeguard Bairrada's native grapes during the 1980s and '90s, when many growers were abandoning them in favour of international varieties. A difference of conviction in farming prompted her to strike out by herself, establishing one of Portugal's few biodynamic estates – a bold move in a region still coming into its own.

That independent streak runs straight through everything Pato and Wouters do. They favour Burgundy bottles over the squared shoulders of Bordeaux, and you taste the difference in intent: elegance and restraint are their true north. When I visited, Wouters poured 'Nossa Calcário' after more than a decade in bottle, alongside lobster in a tarragon broth – a dish as saline and finely judged as the wine. In Bairrada, patience is less a virtue than a tradition.

9

Barbadillo Criadera Selection Palo Cortado en Rama
Drink This Before Everyone Else Catches On

Region
Sanlúcar de Barrameda, Spain

Grape
Palomino Fino

Price
●○○○○

ABV
19%

Food
Sherry is a special food wine, equally at home with challenging octopus stews, ramen, or even a humble cheese toastie.

Right Armando Guerra

Next spread Taberna der Guerrita, Sanlúcar de Barrameda

Armando Guerra's Sanlúcar de Barrameda wine bar and shop, Taberna der Guerrita, stands as a shrine to the town's twin obsessions: Sherry and seafood. Alongside local delicacies such as its *pulpo grotesco* ('grotesque octopus') – the most austere cephalopod dish imaginable, left uncleaned, roughly chopped and boiled in seawater, as fishermen have done for generations – you'll find one of the world's most exciting collections of Sherries. Impossibly scarce Manzanillas and tiny, limited bottlings from ancient Amontillado casks line the shelves like Andalusian magic potions, irresistible to the great and the good of fine wine, who are drawn on pilgrimage to the town. Yet Guerra is more than Sanlúcar's genial host and custodian of its vinous lore. Until recently, his day job as cellar master at Barbadillo – one of the region's most important *bodegas* – was just as enriching. Barbadillo's wines are far easier to find than the treasures of Der Guerrita, and their prices still lag conspicuously behind their quality.

Founded in 1821, Bodegas Barbadillo is a family-owned winery producing some six million bottles each year. Stepping through its gates is like going back to another century. Vast regiments of old oak *botas* rise in dim, cool vaults the size of cathedrals, which smell of salt, yeast and time itself. Some of the cellars have walls deliberately missing, exposing their slumbering treasures to the Atlantic coast elements, suggesting a notion of terroir that applies as much to where in the *bodega* a barrel is aged as to where the grapes are grown. Drawing both affordable releases and rarities from young and ancient *botas*, and playing a central role in the region's reinvention as a maker of Vinos de Pasto (unfortified table wine), this is a winery deeply steeped in the past yet firmly thinking about the future.

MAS TIENE, SINO AQUEL

Butron

Left Dishes at Taberna der Guerrita, Sanlúcar de Barrameda, including 'grotesque octopus'

Barbadillo makes an excellent Palo Cortado, a rare style of Sherry that begins life as a delicate Fino before losing its protective layer of yeast (flor). Exposed to oxygen, the wine deepens in colour and complexity, developing savoury, nutty layers. Aged for more than ten years, it can feel enigmatic at first. But give it a moment, and it soon wins you over. I came to Palo Cortado the way I've come to a lot of good wines: through a friend – Mick Dean – who knew better than I did. I can still picture the moment in his London kitchen when its brothy, leathery, salted-caramel flavours ping-ponged across my taste buds, helped along by smoked almonds. One sip and I was hooked.

This Palo Cortado is bottled *en rama*, straight from the cask, with little or no filtration. Nothing has been polished away, and it shows. It's an invigorating way to begin a meal – the kind of wine that reminds you why Sherry once held a place of honour at the table, and still should at this price.

10

Barraco 'Bianco G'
Leaving Would Have Been Easier

Region
Sicily, Italy

Grape
Grillo

Price
●●○○○

ABV
13.5–14%

Food
Grilled swordfish with olive oil, lemon, capers and oregano – the wine's weight and salinity matching the fish's meaty, oily texture.

Marsala is a place many people gave up on long ago. Fortified wine, industrial sludge, a reputation dragged through the dirt for decades. If you were serious, you left – north, or to Etna – and made something safe and exportable. Nino Barraco didn't. Following the example of Marco De Bartoli, who helped re-establish artisanal winemaking in the town, Barraco stayed put and focused on dry, unfortified table wines at a moment when almost everyone else had written Marsala off as a lost cause. No fortification. No shortcuts. Just grapes, place and disciplined low-intervention winemaking.

Barraco works with undervalued native varieties such as Grillo, Zibibbo and Catarratto, treating the grapes with a seriousness long denied them. His deep golden 'Bianco G', from pure Grillo, is richly textured and poised, with notes of almond and salted green apple, leading to a long, mouthwatering finish. Its more mature sibling 'Altogrado' shows how far the grape can go: aged for seven years in old chestnut casks, it is deeper in colour and more structured, with notes of citrus peel, spice and *tarte Tatin*, alongside a faint echo of old, unfortified Marsala, finishing bone-dry.

These are wines of real character – brilliant, austere and occasionally challenging. They don't flatter; they demand attention. Making wine this way allows nowhere to hide. Making it in Marsala, when leaving would have been easier, follows the same logic.

11

Marco De Bartoli Marsala Superiore Oro 'Vigna la Miccia'

Sicily's Silent Assassin (Served by the Glass)

Region
Sicily, Italy

Grape
Grillo

Price
●●●○○

ABV
18.5–19%

Food
Serve it with a wedge of aged pecorino or a not-too-sweet chocolate dessert.

Marsala is a dangerous wine to develop a taste for. Not 'I-drank-too-much-rosé-at-lunch' dangerous – *real* dangerous. The kind that sneaks up on you, wraps an arm around your shoulder, and whispers, "Come on, just one more." When I first got tangled up with 1988 Marco De Bartoli Vergine Riserva, our old head sommelier Nico – equal parts enabler and co-conspirator – knew exactly what he was doing. He'd drift over at the end of every dinner with an open bottle and that smug, knowing grin that said, "You're not getting out of here so easy."

And who could blame him? The stuff is glorious: rich, spiced and saline, with that deep umami thrum this part of western Sicily knows how to conjure. It's not a dessert wine; it's a final act, a curtain drop, the moment in the night when everything tastes better, looks better, feels better. The problem, of course, is the morning after. This wine – this moreish, oxidative fabulousness – doesn't go quietly. And you realise too late that it is rarely a perfect way to begin the next day.

Marsala has long been written off as cooking wine, but when made with integrity it is a sophisticated, fortified style. Its modern-day story begins in 1773, when a Liverpudlian merchant named John Woodhouse arrived in the town and recognised a familiar sight: barrels stacked in a Sherry-like solera system. He smelled opportunity and began shipping the wine home. Before too long, Marsala became the darling of the British drinking classes.

But tastes are fickle, and by the mid-20th century Marsala's popularity had waned. Industrial production took hold, and its cheap, sugared output was deemed fit mainly for deglazing pans. That is, until Marco De Bartoli decided his hometown's signature wine deserved better. Born into a commercial Marsala dynasty, he could easily have coasted. Instead, in the late 1970s he walked away from the family firm and began using his grandfather's wines as blueprints.

De Bartoli set about rebuilding Marsala's reputation from the ground up. He focused on Grillo – a grape capable of carrying both Sicily's heat and the oxidative demands of extended ageing – lowering yields, hand-selecting grapes and fermenting with wild yeasts, convinced that such things mattered. De Bartoli is now the benchmark against which all Marsala is measured. And although I still love that 1988, the real assassin at Noble Rot is the more modestly priced Marsala Superiore Oro 'Vigna la Miccia', which we've served by the glass for years. It sits among the great sweet wines of the world – proper, taste bud-tingling stuff. Pair it with chocolate, and everything else fades into the background.

12

Paolo Bea 'Rosso de Véo'
Nothing Added, Nothing Taken Away

Below Giampiero Bea, Umbria

Region
Umbria, Italy

Grape
Sagrantino

Price
●●●●○

ABV
14–14.5%

Food
Pasta, hearty stews or a formidable joint of meat – this wine takes them in its stride.

Driving in rural Italy has its own rules – ones that rarely align with the visitor's expectations. Roads appear to wander of their own accord, bending towards olive groves, then slipping between stone walls built long before the automobile was imagined. In Umbria, these paths seem especially certain of their own logic. And so, should you find yourself in the ancient market square of Montefalco, that hilltop town of such precipitous altitude that your ears pop as you ascend, I offer a friendly piece of advice: resist the shortcut.

I learned this on my way to visit Giampiero Bea of Azienda Agricola Paolo Bea, who has long embodied the best of Italian natural wine. What looked, at first glance, like a discreet backstreet soon revealed itself to be a narrowing path. Picture a wedge of pecorino sliced thinner and thinner until you realise the joke is on you and your rental car. There was nothing to do but reverse – carefully, almost meditatively – up the steep incline we had just descended. It was the kind of intimate trial that travel sometimes demands, reminding us that we are guests in a land arranged by other hands.

Noble Rot photographer Ben McMahon still recalls that retreat with affectionate disbelief. Just as readily, he remembers the Paolo Bea reds waiting for us at the top of the hill: muscular Sagrantinos, shaped by altitude, long ferments and a conviction that wine should be generated, not made. Giampiero Bea, an architect-turned-*vigneron* mentored by Giuseppe Quintarelli, Stanko Radikon and Joško Gravner, transformed his family's cow-farming estate into one of Italy's most soulful wineries. He defied Montefalco's tradition of sweet *passito* to craft dry Sagrantino, following the philosophy "nothing added, nothing taken away".

That may sound like the kind of monkish mantra you'd hear in a mountain hermitage, but in practice it's brutal work – hours of letting nature do what it does, and refusing every shortcut that might make life easier. He barely uses sulphur and filters nothing. The proof's right there in the bottle: a powdery texture, with the chew of Sagrantino's thick skin, signalling that this wasn't messed with. 'Rosso de Véo' is the first step into Bea's world, drawn from younger vines. As an earlier-drinking *rosso*, it's more accessible than the estate's grander single-vineyard Sagrantino bottlings, such as 'Cerrete' or 'Pagliaro', yet it speaks in the same voice.

It's a wine of real character – rustic yet disarmingly honest, powerful but never heavy. It has the structure to age gracefully, yet offers immediate pleasure. In the end, our Montefalco experience was instructive. Roads, like wines, ask us to slow down and meet them on their terms. And when we do, the rewards – whether a beautifully made red or getting the hire car back to the airport in one piece – feel all the more satisfying.

13-14

Below Fête du Beaujolais, Noble Rot, Lamb's Conduit Street

Domaine Chapel Beaujolais Villages

Region
Beaujolais, France

Grape
Gamay

Price
●●○○○

ABV
12.5%

Food
Gamay's bright acidity and gentle tannins make it incredibly versatile – just as good with pizza or *pâté de campagne* as it is with grilled fish or bavette.

BEAUJOLAIS
The Grape That Loves Good Company

There's one day each year when our Bloomsbury restaurant feels less like a dining room and more like a medieval village square: Fête du Beaujolais. On the third Thursday of November, we open the doors wide and let the spirit of Gamay spill out onto the street. Contributors to *Noble Rot* magazine, friends, neighbours and assorted hedonists gather for a long lunch that happily drifts into evening. One of our favourite chefs or restaurants takes over the stoves, while outside a small band of Beaujolais growers pour the fruits of their hillsides. For one day, Gamay calls all the shots – and on Lamb's Conduit Street, in the cold autumn air, wine lovers talking, laughing, drinking and smoking are living proof that fine wine is made to be shared.

Among those growers, David and Michele Chapel of Domaine Chapel have become regulars. They belong to a younger generation of Beaujolais *vignerons* who grew up in the wake of producers such as Marcel Lapierre and Jean Foillard – growers who kicked against industrial production and proved that Beaujolais didn't need enzymes or laboratory gloss to thrive. Chapel's Beaujolais Villages is exactly the sort of wine you want on a day like this: fresh, supple, modestly priced, and gone almost as soon as it's poured. It doesn't ask for attention or reverence. It just does its job – which is to be drunk, happily, with friends.

Gamay is a grape made for good company. In Lyon, the city that lies a few miles south of its heartland, they say there are three rivers – the Rhône, the Saône and a third that flows through the glasses of its *bouchons* and bars: Beaujolais. Given the vineyards' proximity, it's easy to see why. Beaujolais Cru – wines from one of its 12 communes – typically shows bright freshness, moderate tannins and modest alcohol, making it a lighter red that is best enjoyed young, with a slight chill, offering juicy drinkability with a gently savoury edge.

ATLANTIC

Domaine Coudert Fleurie 'Clos de la Roilette Cuvée Tardive'

Region
Beaujolais, France

Grape
Gamay

Price
●●○○○

ABV
13%

At the more age-worthy end of the category, Domaine Coudert Fleurie 'Clos de la Roilette Cuvée Tardive' is a special bottling made from winemaker Alain Coudert's oldest vines. He calls it *tardive* (late) not because it's harvested late, but because he believes it deserves to be drunk with greater maturity than most Fleuries, a village famed for floral, ethereal reds of early charm. The name 'Clos de la Roilette' harks back to a previous owner, Émile Crozet, who, affronted when his estate was reclassified as Fleurie rather than the grander Moulin-à-Vent in the 1920s, named the wine after his racehorse, Roilette, and never forgave the authorities. For good measure, he swore never to sell a bottle in France, sending every case to England, Germany and Switzerland instead.

Coudert says his old vines, grown on well-exposed soils on the border of Moulin-à-Vent, sit on clay-rich ground rather than the granite typical of the area, giving 'Cuvée Tardive' its extra substance. If you want to explore the finer side of Beaujolais – beyond the 'glou-glou' styles (the joyfully thirst-quenching wines meant to be drunk young) – this is the bottle to reach for. Unlike red Burgundy to the north, where top vineyards fetch thousands per bottle, it's remarkable that one of Beaujolais's finest wines can still be had for under £30. Beaujolais Cru remains among the most underrated wines on the planet – versatile, joyous and unpretentious. A truly democratic pleasure, best enjoyed in abundance with friends.

Left Alain Coudert, Domaine Coudert, Fleurie

15

Domaine Belargus 'Ronceray'
Where a Hundred Years Begins

Region
Loire Valley, France

Grape
Chenin Blanc

Price
●●○○○

ABV
13.5%

Food
This feels right with a lovely piece of pork with crackling. The wine has shape, and it wants something with structure in return.

The road from boardroom to vineyard is well worn, but once in a while, someone walks it with real conviction. Ivan Massonnat is proof of how a second act in wine can be a calling fulfilled with a deep respect for artisanal culture rather than a mediocre vanity project. After a prosperous run as an entrepreneur, initially his eyes turned towards Burgundy. What wine lover hasn't dreamed of owning a few rows of vines in Chambertin? But fate, as it so often does, had other plans. A chance meeting with Jo Pithon, one of the Loire Valley's most steadfast champions, pulled him westward. What began as a business deal – Ivan's purchase of Jo's Domaine Pithon-Paillé – turned into something more interesting: a meeting of minds.

The newly christened Domaine Belargus took root in Anjou's rolling hills with Jo serving as Ivan's adviser. Centuries ago, this was a serious wine region, but the French Revolution changed everything. Fine wine, so long entwined with the Church and the aristocracy, became tarnished by association. For the next two centuries, Anjou's ambitions faded, and the region made do with rustic wines. Now, as part of what Ivan calls "a hundred-year plan", Belargus and a handful of like-minded domaines are reclaiming the region's ambition – once again making it a place where great wines grow. In a range of terroir-specific cuvées, worthy of any Burgundian producer, they show that Chenin Blanc can speak as clearly of place as Chardonnay. Taste with Jo and Ivan and talk always drifts back to the land – to schist, limestone, pudding stones and the river.

Chenin Blanc is a shapeshifter. It built the Loire's reputation on sweet wines such as Quarts de Chaume; now it's delivering dry, nervy bottles that feel perfectly attuned to how we drink today. What makes Chenin distinctive is that the fruit is often secondary to texture and minerality (sensations of stone, salt, and more). On the Loire's schist and limestone soils, it's tight, upright, acidic – built more like a load-bearing wall than a bowl of fruit. Drawn from an enviable collection of vineyards – Treilles, Clos des Bonnes Blanches, and sites in Savennières and Quarts de Chaume – assembled by Jo over the course of his career, alongside more recent acquisitions, Domaine Belargus has become one of the most ambitious projects in the Loire.

A good place to begin is 'Ronceray' – from vines on the hill of Quarts de Chaume, the Loire's only Grand Cru. That it does not qualify for the appellation – being dry rather than sweet – reveals less about the wine than about the rigidity of the rules that govern it. It's a Chenin of power and tension that feels both rooted in history and entirely of the present.

16

Bérêche et Fils Champagne Brut Réserve NV
Champagne Is a Wine. Discuss

Region
Champagne, France

Grapes
Chardonnay, Pinot Noir, Pinot Meunier

Price
●●●●○

ABV
12–12.5%

Food
Drink it with a simple roast chicken with lemon and herbs – or even with buttermilk fried chicken. But more than that, it rewards informality. Don't wait for a toast. Open it because dinner's ready.

Most of us grew up with a distorted idea of what Champagne really is. Glitzy and expensive, but ultimately a little sour and hollow. The Champenois did a remarkable job of marketing it as a category apart, too precious to be treated as wine, reserved exclusively for celebration. Then a new generation of growers – Raphaël and Vincent Bérêche among them – changed everything. Not the idea of Champagne as something precious, or as the perfect companion to life's joyful moments. But the notion that it is only that. They showed us that Champagne, at its heart, is wine – and that by farming thoughtfully and making it authentically, it can be far more satisfying than the vast industrial cuvées and polished slogans of the *Grandes Marques*.

Bérêche et Fils Champagne Brut Réserve NV is a seriously fine Champagne: graceful, versatile and unfailingly good value. From Ludes on the northern slopes of the Montagne de Reims, this wine balances racy acidity with a salt-citrus-chalky vinosity that works as beautifully at the table as it does on its own. It's the kind of bottle that makes sense almost anywhere – lunch outside on the first warm day of spring, a bar before a show, or simply because you're alive, a little thirsty, and there are a couple of glasses to hand. I've got a soft spot for Bérêche Brut Réserve NV not just at the start of a long meal, but at the end of it too. After the reds have had their say, a glass of fizz does wonders – it clears the head, sharpens the conversation, and sends everyone off smiling. With a cheese course, it proves a most happy and adaptable companion.

17-18 BOURGOGNE
Isn't Supposed to Be This Good

Benjamin Leroux Bourgogne Blanc

Region
Burgundy, France

Grape
Chardonnay

Price
●●○○○

ABV
12.5–13.5%

Denis Mortet Bourgogne Rouge 'Cuvée de Noble Souche'

Region
Burgundy, France

Grape
Pinot Noir

Price
●●●○○

ABV
13%

Food
Fish cooked on the bone with butter for the white; chargrilled quail with a green salad for the red. After that, trust your instincts – both wines are remarkably accommodating.

We've always sold more Burgundy at Noble Rot restaurants than any other wine. From truckloads of restorative Mâcon to the occasional bottle of mythical Musigny, Burgundy is the reason we got into this business – and the reason we remain. Yes, prices have climbed, sometimes beyond what most of us consider reasonable. But here's the part that often gets overlooked: improved farming and more sensitive cellar work, combined with rising temperatures that have made grape ripening more consistent, have transformed the wines by which most people now know the region. Today's entry-level AOC Bourgogne reds and whites are the best I've ever known them – alive, transparent, and often more compelling than many Premiers Crus were a generation ago.

Burgundy is often explained as a pyramid, but that makes it sound more rigid than it really is. At the top are the Grand Crus, sites that, year after year, have shown an almost stubborn ability to ripen fruit. Just below them are the Premiers Crus – vineyards of distinction, sometimes separated from their more famous neighbours by nothing more than a stone wall or a change in slope. Then come the village wines, bottles that often taste unmistakably of where they come from: Nuits-Saint-Georges, Chambolle-Musigny, and the rest. And finally there is Bourgogne, made from grapes grown on less privileged land across an area stretching from Chablis in the north to Beaujolais in the south. The word can make people think of compromise. It shouldn't. At its best, Bourgogne is deeply satisfying.

I could name plenty of domaines turning out beautiful Bourgogne, but I'm thinking here about two *vignerons* who are now making some of the best wines of their careers. In Beaune, the medieval town at the heart of Burgundy's trade, Benjamin Leroux makes a white Bourgogne of charm and assurance. It's delicious young, but it's also built to go the distance if you've got the patience. The last bottle I opened, ten years on from vintage, was very much alive: fresh and floral, with a suggestion of roasted nuts and crushed fennel seeds. It came from vines in Meursault, and it tasted like it knew it.

Further north, in Gevrey-Chambertin, the Denis Mortet Bourgogne Rouge 'Cuvée de Noble Souche' is one of the most convincing Pinot Noirs I've tasted at any level. Bright and lifted, with real energy, its sweet black fruit is framed, as in all great Burgundy, by a savoury depth. I've drunk Mortet's rare Grand Cru Chambertin. It's a lovely wine – but when the introduction to his range is this good, do you care?

19

G.B. Burlotto Verduno Pelaverga

My Other Wine Is a Barolo

Region
Piedmont, Italy

Grape
Pelaverga Piccolo

Price
●●○○○

ABV
13–14%

Food
Pelaverga works with Piedmontese specialities such as *vitello tonnato* as happily as it does with quiche or a Caesar salad.

Right Fabio Alessandria, G.B. Burlotto, Verduno

Next spread Piedmont vineyards

Fabio Alessandria may be best known for making G.B. Burlotto's 'Monvigliero', one of Barolo's most sensual wines. But taste with him in his cellar, amid the fog-shrouded backstreets of Verduno, and the conversation turns at the mention of Pelaverga – the humble local grape that his grandfather Ignazio Burlotto once rescued from the brink of extinction. It's the bottle he admits he reaches for most often, and it's easy to see why. Pelaverga has a light step and a wide orbit, slipping naturally into places at the table that Barolo's heavyweights never can. Pale ruby in colour, this gentle red is acutely responsive to place – and season.

What's remarkable is that when Fabio's parents – Marina Burlotto and Giuseppe Alessandria – replanted Pelaverga with a few friends from a low of just 3ha, they did so in an era obsessed with muscle and extraction. Pelaverga offered none of that. A generation on, a once-forgotten variety slips easily into the modern moment – fresh, lifted and as true to Verduno as Nebbiolo itself. Today, Fabio tends three of the roughly 30ha of Pelaverga clinging to the hills around the village. Tasting across vintages, Pelaverga shows a gently spiced, red-fruited profile – think cherries, strawberries, cranberries, violets and herbs – carried on an airy frame. In warmer years it speaks in a riper, more fruit-forward voice; in cooler ones it opens like a flower, all perfume and nuance.

Pelaverga has weathered the new rhythms of the climate better than many varieties: warm summers have given it greater flesh, while in colder, rainier vintages it could show greenness. Fabio ages the wine for around six or seven months before release and usually opens it within five years of harvest – a wine meant for early drinking pleasure, as he says, "on a picnic, or with a light lunch or dinner", rather than tucked away for decades. If Burlotto's majestic Barolos are bottles you uncork for life's fanfares, Pelaverga is the everyday jewel in its cellar – a treasure that curious wine lovers should seek out.

20

Weingut Clemens Busch 'Vom Roten Schiefer' Riesling

The Steep Price of Greatness

Region
Mosel Valley, Germany

Grape
Riesling

Price
●●○○○

ABV
11–11.5%

Food
The wine's guava and passion fruit, with a touch of smoky slate, are made for pork fat and aromatic spice.

Marienburg is one of those places that make you question the sanity – and then admire the stubbornness – of the people who farm them. Perched high above the Mosel, it unfolds as a vertigo-inducing cascade of slate slopes, pitched at an angle that makes you instinctively lean back just to take it in. This is not a vineyard that yields easily. Nothing here can be rushed or mechanised; every task is done by hand, every decision paid for in sweat – and, one suspects, in physiotherapist's bills.

Clemens Busch chose to expand the site he inherited from his father not because it was forgiving, but because he recognised what it might become. Farming old vines with uncompromising care, he has articulated the identity of Marienburg – alongside other steep parcels such as Rothenpfad and Nonnengarten – with clarity. Among the first in Germany to embrace organic and biodynamic viticulture, and to commit to dry Rieslings, he was already there when the climate shifted. The result is wines of such character that they now rank among the country's finest.

Riesling 'Vom Roten Schiefer' is, in essence, Busch's village-level wine, drawn from younger vines rooted in red slate on Rothenpfad and Nonnengarten. If grey slate is the backbone of the Middle Mosel – dominant across the estate – and blue slate the rarer strain, associated with delicacy, then red tends to be more expressive in its youth. It introduces a more exotic note – guava and passion fruit – into Busch's familiar register of wet stone and smoke.

He makes these soil distinctions tangible by sealing his bottles with different-coloured capsules, each signalling the slate that defines the site. Marienburg, however, is the name that resonates most powerfully, thanks to Busch's work over decades. If 'Vom Roten Schiefer' appeals, 'Marienburg Rothenpfad' GG Riesling Trocken – also from red slate – makes the case in full. Yes, it costs nearly twice as much – but a single inhale of its pungent, untamed nose makes clear why Busch chooses steep slopes over open fields.

21

Azienda Agricola Caparsino Chianti Classico Riserva
Wine as Bread, Not Bling

Region
Tuscany, Italy

Grapes
Sangiovese, Canaiolo Nero, Colorino

Price
●●○○○

ABV
13.5–14%

Food
Pappardelle al ragù di cinghiale – rich, slow-cooked boar pasta – is the kind of dish this wine was made for.

Next spread Filippo and Paolo Cianferoni, Caparsa estate, Tuscany

"I like to be a peasant," Paolo Cianferoni tells me when I visit his Caparsa estate in Chianti Classico. "Wine is not just fashion. My philosophy is to produce it as if it were food." And he means it, too. When Cianferoni was growing up in this corner of Tuscany in the 1960s, the area was all but abandoned, and wine was, quite literally, food. A slice of bread, a spoonful of sugar and a few drops of red wine made a typical treat for children. Things are different now. The region is more prosperous, its hills dotted with estates owned by Russians, Austrians, Chinese and English. The influx of money has driven up quality but, under the sway of an army of consultants, it has also fuelled a wave of overblown commercial wines, heavy with new oak and alcohol. At the same time, traditionalists such as Cianferoni continue to champion Sangiovese's delicate characteristics through more sympathetic methods.

Caparsa Chianti Classico Riserva is as old-school as it comes – the antithesis of sterile, technical winemaking. Lush black fruit unfolds into mineral savouriness, supported by fine, powdery tannins and finishing with a flicker of dark-chocolate bitterness. I love that Cianferoni isn't afraid of a little volatile acidity from traditional long ageing, seasoning the perfume with a prickle of balsamic. If you find yourself in Chianti Classico, visiting Caparsa is a refreshingly straightforward experience, far removed from the choreographed tastings and architectural bravado of larger estates. And while drinking well for next to nothing has become nearly impossible in Britain or America, Cianferoni still sells his everyday wines by the 54-litre demi-john from the cellar door – for people who don't collect wine, but simply drink it.

14C
hl.40

22

Tenuta di Carleone 'Uno'
One-Eyed in Tuscany

Region
Tuscany, Italy

Grape
Sangiovese

Price
●●●●○

ABV
13–14%

Food
'Uno' is especially at home with *bistecca alla fiorentina* – a thick T-bone meant for sharing – or *pappardelle al cinghiale*, a rich wild boar ragù. But Sangiovese is a friendly grape that pairs well with an unusually broad range of dishes.

Left Sean O'Callaghan, Tenuta di Carleone, Tuscany

If making wine that matters means taking risks, Sean O'Callaghan is a *vigneron* at ease on the edge. This self-styled *Il Guercio* – Italian for 'the one-eyed man' – grew up in Devon but has long been at home in Tuscany. He learned his craft at the well-regarded Riecine in Chianti Classico, then went out on his own. As winemaker at Tenuta di Carleone, he started shaping fresh, perfumed Sangiovese, with just enough wildness to keep it from becoming too polite. With 'Uno' he selects his favourite barrels from each vintage and releases the wine outside the Chianti Classico appellation, because, of course, rules were not always going to suit him.

Tuscan Sangiovese tends to fall into two camps: one modern – all muscle, oak and alcohol, often bulked out with international grapes; the other paler, more graceful, perfumed and finely drawn. The latter is sometimes described as '*gambelliano*' after the *maestro assaggiatore* Giulio Gambelli, whose palate shaped legends such as 'Le Pergole Torte'. 'Uno', though less than half the price of 'Le Pergole Torte', holds its own: a joyous Italian red, with an easy, disarming sensuality. At my last birthday party I opened jeroboams that, unlike some of the guests, improved as the night wore on.

I adore Sangiovese made with a light touch, producing paler hues, fine-grained tannins and a Pinot-like spectrum of strawberry and cherry. O'Callaghan achieves this by keeping the juice gently in contact with the skins and stems for longer than usual, favouring freshness and aroma over excessive extraction. This approach can also produce vinegary aromas – known as volatile acidity – that most wineries go to great lengths to avoid. In excess it spoils a wine, but in tiny amounts it adds complexity to many of the world's most captivating reds. Gambelli himself disliked the modern obsession with stripping it out at all costs, believing that a small amount added charm. O'Callaghan walks a similar path, poised between rapture and ruin.

23

Château Les Carmes Haut-Brion
Bordeaux, Reconsidered

Region
Bordeaux, France

Grapes
Cabernet Sauvignon, Cabernet Franc, Merlot

Price
●●●●○

ABV
13.5%

Food
Best decanted for a couple of hours and served with a rib of beef or slow-cooked shoulder of lamb.

Previous pages Château Les Carmes Haut-Brion, Bordeaux

Bordeaux didn't just fall off the map; it polished and priced itself out of relevance. Not so long ago, those Cru Classé châteaux sat at the centre of the wine universe, their names uttered with something approaching religious devotion. Generations of British drinkers snapped them up *en primeur*, at generous discounts, stacked them away like canned goods for the apocalypse, and passed the habit on to their kids. Then Bordeaux did what empires tend to do: it started believing its own press. Prices crept up, wines got slicker, shinier, safer – buffed up by consultants chasing scores instead of pleasure. Somewhere in that process, the soul went missing.

Meanwhile, a younger generation learned to drink differently. They came up on Beaujolais Crus, on cloudy orange wines, on bottles that tasted fresh and alive and didn't require 20 years in a cellar they didn't own to be enjoyable. So when they see a bottle of Bordeaux, they don't feel awe or desire. They feel nothing at all. And indifference, as any *vigneron* will tell you, is the kiss of death.

Yet search the market and you will find something remarkable: mature Bordeaux has become one of the great bargains in fine wine. While 25-year-old top-tier Burgundy vanishes into the vaults of oligarchs, clarets of a similar age – brimming with the gentle savouriness long ageing can coax – sit patiently on merchants' shelves, asking to be bought by someone who cares. Often, these wines are priced similarly to new releases. Which means that, to survive, Bordeaux has to get back to what made it successful in the first place: offering characterful, reliable wines at attainable prices – like Château Les Carmes Haut-Brion.

Prices at Château Les Carmes Haut-Brion have risen in recent years. Even so, it remains reasonably priced for a special-occasion red that can be enjoyed young and dares to do things differently. For a start, it has a high proportion of fragrant Cabernet Franc, a grape more associated with Saint-Émilion than Graves, where the estate is located. The fruit is picked early and only partially destemmed before being fermented using a unique infusion method.

While whole-cluster fermentations are common in Burgundy, few if anyone in Bordeaux had used them for decades before Les Carmes Haut-Brion revived the practice. Lending freshness and lift to the perfume, this approach highlights Graves' signature aromas of warm brick and blackcurrant. The result is a wine with fine tannins and restrained alcohol – averaging 13.5% ABV, compared with the 15% found at some neighbouring estates. Château Les Carmes Haut-Brion is a rare Bordeaux that marries innovation with authenticity and tradition.

24

Chanterêves Bourgogne 'Miarlons du Bas' Aligoté
Serious Wine for Hungry People

Region
Burgundy, France

Grape
Aligoté

Price
●●●○○

ABV
13.5%

Food
Perfect for a long, languid lunch of Burgundian classics – *escargots*, *jambon persillé*, roast chicken, Époisses, *tarte fine* – followed by a nap.

For those who care as much about eating as drinking, lighter wines have a particular virtue: they encourage another bite and quench thirst. They refresh rather than overwhelm, keeping pace with a meal without slowing it down with heft or alcohol. Here, Aligoté excels. Its price, too, usually remains sane by Burgundy standards: some of the most satisfying bottles are among the least expensive, while plenty of costly ones disappoint. A carefully made Aligoté from a thoughtful grower can give more pleasure than a Grand Cru Chardonnay from a less attentive hand. What matters is how a wine lives at the table: with food, with friends, across a meal.

Aligoté was once co-planted with Chardonnay in top Burgundy vineyards such as Les Monts Luisants, contributing to serious, age-worthy whites. Its reputation later slipped, dragged down by thin, acidic wines from poorly farmed vines in the wrong places. It became the everyday fuel of Burgundy's bars and bistros, often poured with a dash of crème de cassis to make a kir, softening its edges. In recent years, a new generation of growers has returned to it with intent. Today, Aligoté can express place as clearly as any wine in Burgundy.

Chanterêves is the husband-and-wife partnership of Guillaume Bott and Tomoko Kuriyama, with a particular focus on Aligoté, which they bottle in five distinct expressions, each compelling in its own way. 'Miarlons du Bas' shows what the grape can be at its best: apple and citrus, a stony clarity, and a density few would expect. This is the kind of white Burgundy that keeps the gourmand alert at the table, reaching for another bite, another glass.

25

Domaine Marie-Thérèse Chappaz 'Coteaux de Plamont'

A Country That Keeps Its Treasures to Itself

Region
Valais, Switzerland

Grape
Fendant

Price
●●●●○

ABV
11.7–12.5%

Food
Raclette, in heroic quantities.

Left Marie-Thérèse Chappaz, Valais

Next spread Chappaz's 'Combe d'Enfer' ('Valley of Hell') vineyard in Valais

Switzerland makes some remarkable wines – wines of vertigo and sweat, priced like Rolexes. But try getting your hands on a bottle. The Swiss drink nearly all of it themselves, and they're not losing sleep over whether you or I ever taste the stuff. They're a prosperous bunch, and when a wine is good, they simply keep it and drink it. Export? That's a courtesy, not a business plan.

Located in Valais, Marie-Thérèse Chappaz's winemaking has more in common with rock climbing than farming. You don't stroll into her vineyards; you cling to them. Every vine looks like it was planted by someone hanging off a rope. It's agriculture, yes, but the kind that requires a harness and a good relationship with gravity. And the only way in and out of those high-altitude parcels like 'Coteaux de Plamont', where this Fendant is grown, is by riding her cable car. It's less a means of transport than a dare. You grip the sides, pray to whatever god oversees mountain viticulture, and hope the thing decides to stay on the wire.

Known as Chasselas just across the border in France, Fendant is the grape behind more forgettable après-ski wines than anyone cares to remember. In Valais, though, raised with care, it sheds that reputation and has real texture and refinement. It's also the classic companion to *raclette*, that national sacrament of potatoes drowned in molten cheese; if you haven't had the two together, give yourself the chance to understand why the Swiss try to keep it to themselves. Chappaz makes four biodynamic Fendants, each one capable of making anyone rethink what they thought they knew about this supposedly simple grape.

'Coteaux de Plamont' is a pure, restrained white wine whose slate-edged finish slices straight through molten cheese. Proof that, in the right hands, even the humblest grape can climb.

26

Chartreuse
Perfume You Can Drink

Region
Le Massif de la Chartreuse, France

Grapes
Yellow Chartreuse is grape spirit – likely Ugni Blanc or Colombard; Green Chartreuse is made from beetroot

Price
●●●○○

ABV
Yellow 43%, Green 55%

Food
Drink it by itself. It already contains a mountain, a monastery and several centuries of conviction. That's plenty.

Right The less said, the better

Next spread The Monastery of Grande Chartreuse, France

Okay, fine – Chartreuse isn't a wine. But it shows up where wine culture lives: late dinners, stained tablecloths, tired winemakers and bad decisions that feel very good at the time. That alone makes it worth talking about. Chartreuse's story, in fact, centres on religious fanatics who actually do some good in the world. Fundamentalists who, rather than seeking out gnarly martyrdom, make people's lives better. Some four centuries ago, their forebears began distilling an elixir meant to heal the sick – and, if truth be told, to keep the monastery solvent. Centuries later, that same potion has evolved into the Green and Yellow Chartreuses that inspire a devoted following today.

Their story encompasses vows of silence, exile undertaken to escape state persecution and a recipe guarded with near-mystical secrecy. But above all, it's about a drink that smells so divine you could dab it behind your ears instead of perfume. Say what you will about the decline of Christianity – any faith capable of creating a potion this perfect deserves to live forever. God bless you, Chartreuse.

Chartreuse is, variously, a silent order of Carthusian monks, a mountain range in south-eastern France, and – as Quentin Tarantino has it in *Death Proof* – 'the only liqueur so good they named a colour after it'. Indeed, the first time I drank it, it was so unlike anything I'd ever tasted that it felt less like discovering another shade of green and more like stumbling upon a new primary colour. Thick, sweet and spicy, the young Chartreuse poured at the end of a dinner in a Lyonnais *bouchon* was simple but delicious. Only later, when I encountered older bottles, did I begin to grasp its mind-boggling array of aromas and flavours. Distilled from dried Alpine herbs and exotic spices, it smells the way the foothills of the Misty Mountains in Middle-earth look at dawn.

ZONE
DE SILENCE

CHARTREUSE

Left Chartreuse Liqueur du 9ème Centenaire

The only ingredient I know with certainty that Chartreuse contains is lemon balm. Even the few lay workers at the Aiguenoire distillery are deliberately kept from the details; they receive numbered sacks of pre-measured herbs and spices from the Monastery of Grande Chartreuse which are steeped in 96% alcohol – beetroot-based for the Green, grape-based for the Yellow – with a splash of water added before distillation. At 55% alcohol, the Green is fresher and more piercing than the softer, sweeter Yellow, at 43%. My favourites are Green Chartreuse VEP (exceptionally prolonged ageing) and the Liqueur du 9ème Centenaire. They're best taken neat, at cellar temperature, in wine glasses frosted for 20 minutes in the freezer.

Old bottles of Chartreuse, some reaching back into the last century, have become objects of obsession. The liqueur keeps almost indefinitely once opened, so even a half-drunk bottle unearthed in an old bar or inherited from a long-forgotten drinks cabinet can be unexpectedly valuable – one of the few liqueurs that improves with age. Since the early 1990s, a six-digit code has been printed on the side of Chartreuse screw caps to indicate when each bottle was released. Rather cryptically, you can work out the year by adding the first three digits to 1084 – the founding year of the Carthusian order – while the last three numbers reveal the exact day of bottling.

If I've learned anything about the enigmatic residents of the Monastery of Grande Chartreuse, it's that they're bona fide marketing geniuses as well.

27

Château Climens
You're Wrong About Sweet Wine

Region
Bordeaux, France

Grape
Sémillon

Price
●●●○○

ABV
13–14.5%

Food
Foie gras and Roquefort are the orthodox pairings for Château Climens, and for good reason. One of its great forgotten pleasures is with oysters – a Victorian habit worth reviving.

In sweet white wine, the hierarchy has long been simple: Château d'Yquem – and then everything else. Made from the finest parcels of Sauternes, 40km south-east of Bordeaux, for generations this liquid gold has been romanticised and venerated, poured for kings, queens and prime ministers as if siphoned straight from heaven's cellar. It is remarkably long-lived, and 50- to 100-year-old vintages from a cooler time – when the wines were less sweet and carried greater mineral freshness – rank among the most amazing things I've drunk. But the truth is that in the richer style of more recent years, particularly in its youth, there is little to separate Yquem from other leading châteaux. For my money, Château Climens in neighbouring Barsac has long offered similarly luscious pleasure – without the need for genuflection, or the price tag.

Château Climens is both labour-intensive and risky to make, its existence shaped by the interplay of misty mornings and warm afternoons in the vineyards, conditions that encourage a capricious fungus called *Botrytis cinerea* (also known as 'noble rot'). This fungus shrivels the Sémillon grapes, which in turn concentrates their sugars and acidity – the essential raw material for the production of great sweet wines. Noble rot rarely develops evenly through the vineyards, so pickers have to comb the bunches with near-surgical precision, returning several times to harvest only perfectly botrytised berries. Yields are minute, and in some years *Botrytis* may fail to appear at all.

But when everything goes to plan, the results can be extraordinary. Beginning life as a pale straw-coloured white, then deepening to radiant yellow, and eventually darkening to toffee brown, these wines deliver some of the most distinctive and gourmand flavours in the world of drink – apricots, peaches, marmalade and crème brûlée, all shot through with saffron, beeswax and truffle. We live in a modern world saturated with refined sugar, and somewhere along the way many of us have lost our appetite for sweet wine. In leaner eras, when good food was scarce, wines like these must have seemed miraculous. Open a bottle of Château Climens and you'll understand why.

28

Below Dani Jiménez-Landi and Fernando García, Sierra de Gredos

Region
Sierra de Gredos, Spain

Grape
Garnacha

Price
●○○○○

ABV
14–14.5%

Food
Simply perfect with lamb chops, pink in the middle.

Comando G 'La Bruja de Rozas'
Start at the Bottom, Drink Like the Top

Dani Jiménez-Landi once told me that Spain was like a castle that had been locked for years, its treasures only just beginning to be discovered by the world. I nodded, pretending I understood. I didn't. Not really. It took years of tastings with the country's younger generation of winemakers – from the salt and rot of Jerez to the rain-soaked Basque Country – for it to sink in. Spain wasn't asleep. It was busy becoming something else while the rest of us were distracted. Somewhere along the way, without asking anyone's permission, it turned into one of the most exciting wine countries on the planet.

Jiménez-Landi and Fernando García are two of the nicest wine obsessives you'll ever meet. Like many of this new wave of Spanish *vignerons*, they started with almost nothing except conviction and a nagging sense that something important had been overlooked. That hunch led them to the Gredos Mountains, west of Madrid – a region scattered with abandoned vineyards, once used to grow grapes for anonymous bulk wine. Under the name Comando G, they now work those same granite slopes to produce Garnachas of startling purity and finesse, from vineyards with names that sound like heavy-metal albums: 'Rumbo al Norte' ('Heading North'), 'Tumba del Rey Moro' ('Tomb of the Moorish King').

Those bottles are made in small quantities and, even when you can find them, can be costly to buy. But 'La Bruja de Rozas', their entry-level wine, captures much of the same spirit at a more accessible price. One of the simplest tricks I know to drink better – and one I return to again and again – is to buy the 'basic' wine from producers like Dani and Fernando, who are obsessed with doing things right. The grand cuvées may be built for the long haul – destined to unfurl their mysteries a decade or two from now, assuming you have the patience – but most of us don't drink that way. 'La Bruja de Rozas' is made for now. For drinking on a Wednesday, without ceremony.

Lighter on its feet but deeply satisfying, it carries that telltale Comando G restraint – nothing added, nothing forced. There's a fleeting nod to their original inspiration, Châteauneuf-du-Pape's iconic Château Rayas (see pp. 214–15), in the cherry-kirsch perfume, but this is no Mediterranean expression. It is Garnacha shaped by mountain light, emblematic of Spain's reinvention.

29-30

André Perret Condrieu 'Chéry'

Region
Northern Rhône Valley, France

Grape
Viognier

Price
●●●●○

ABV
13.5–14%

Below 'Côteaux du Chéry', Condrieu, northern Rhône Valley

François Dumas Condrieu

Region
Northern Rhône Valley, France

Grape
Viognier

Price
●●●○○

ABV
13.5%

Food
Condrieu belongs at the table – with plenty of cream, butter, roast poultry or shellfish.

CONDRIEU
Pleasure without Apology

Condrieu has never been especially interested in behaving itself. Made from Viognier grown on the steep slopes of the Rhône, it is a highly aromatic, opulent white wine – sometimes excessive, always individual, and notoriously difficult to get right. This is not a grape inclined to restraint; it speaks plainly of a place that, with its butter- and cream-rich cuisine, has never felt obliged to compromise. Love it or hate it, it refuses to fade into the background.

Anyone approaching Condrieu armed with modern expectations is likely to be surprised. We're conditioned to revere wines that improve with age – and usually we're right. Condrieu is the exception. It lives in the present tense, lush and fragrant, offering a seductive swirl of stone fruits, honeysuckle and cream, with no interest in waiting its turn. Its greatness lies not in how long it endures, but in how vividly it inhabits the moment in which it is opened.

Condrieu also sits apart from today's fixation on acidity. At a moment when white wines are praised for their tension, it is softer, more generous, unconcerned with fashion. Viognier is not a high-acid grape, yet the best Condrieu never feel slack. Their balance comes from an appetising bitterness – what the Italians call *amarognolo* – that rises from the quartz-rich soils. The structure is built on contrast: richness held in check by mineral restraint.

Condrieu is a tiny appellation, its prices reflecting its scarcity and the back-breaking work required to farm it. For a long while after the Second World War, few seemed to care. The hills were too steep, the terraces too narrow, the labour too hard. Where they could, growers drifted away, selling their parcels and taking factory jobs nearby, in what people grimly came to call Chemical Valley. By 1965, Viognier was nearly extinct: just 8ha remained, all clinging to Condrieu. Two growers refused to let it die, Georges Vernay and Étienne Guigal, and carried on until, in the mid-1980s, the wider world began to recognise that something irreplaceable was at stake.

André Perret's Condrieu 'Chéry' and François Dumas's Condrieu are among my favourites. Perret, a modest grower, farms old vines on the historic Côteaux du Chéry, a slope Emperor Probus famously spared – calling it his "darling hillside" – when ordering the surrounding vineyards torn out. Aged in old oak rather than new – which can smother Viognier – the wine is rich and textural, never tipping into excess. François Dumas, by contrast, produces a low-sulphur expression of Condrieu: refined, less predictable from vintage to vintage, and intended for the table.

31

Frank Cornelissen 'Munjebel' Bianco

The Fall and Rise of Italian White Wine Culture

Region
Mount Etna, Sicily

Grapes
Grecanico Dorato, Carricante

Price
●●●○○

ABV
13–14%

Food
'Munjebel Bianco' cuts cleanly through the richness of spaghetti carbonara, Sicily and Rome briefly speaking the same language at the table.

Right Luigi Veronelli cellar, Bergamo

Luigi Veronelli was a writer and gastronome whose influence reshaped Italian wine. Coming of age after the war, he championed small growers and resisted industrialisation, arguing that respect for place demanded discipline as much as belief. Veronelli died in 2004, yet the cellar he blasted from the rock beneath his villa in Bergamo – still containing some 35,000 immaculately preserved bottles – endures as part of Italy's cultural heritage.

Entering that cellar feels like stepping into a private history of artisanal Italian wine. Closed to the public, it contains bottles that were often acquired directly from growers, and left undisturbed. Many of the tannin-rich reds remain revelatory, from the masters of Piedmont to the country's more out-of-the-way corners. Yet it was the white wines that astonished me most: 'simple' Soaves and Verdicchios from the Marche that, over decades, had evolved into something magnificent.

Today, many of the producers who once made those Soaves and Verdicchios produce generic styles. Relatively few Italian whites possess the authority to stand alongside the finest of France or Spain. Much of this loss of individuality coincided with the rise of consultant oenologists in wineries during the 1990s, when technique increasingly arrived before taste. Yet one white that would unquestionably have earned a place in Luigi Veronelli's personal canon is 'Munjebel' Bianco, made by Frank Cornelissen in Sicily.

At the beginning of the noughties, Cornelissen exchanged his life as a wine merchant in Antwerp for that of a *vigneron* on Mount Etna, driven by an ambition to make what he called "liquid rock" – anti-wines conceived in reaction to the technological styles of the late 1990s. I have followed his work on Etna with fascination. The idea of 'liquid rock' was always seductive, though in those early, zero-sulphur years the results could be uneven, as conviction sometimes outran control.

Cornelissen's whites began life as orange wines, shaped by extended skin contact. Over time, his ambitions shifted towards greater elegance. As his confidence grew, he eventually allowed a trace of sulphur, accepting that fidelity to place sometimes requires restraint rather than refusal. Given that he'd once been regarded as a standard-bearer of the natural wine movement, the decision was controversial. Yet the results say it all. 'Munjebel' Bianco is a fresh, harmonious white, full of apricot, herb and stone-like flavours – a wine shaped by the same seriousness of intent that guided Veronelli himself.

765
766
767
Il Cerasus di
NONINO
KIRSCH
NONINO

32

Craven 'Karibib' Chenin Blanc
Pay Attention

Region
Stellenbosch, South Africa

Grape
Chenin Blanc

Price
●●○○○

ABV
13%

Food
Sea bass on the grill, brushed with decent olive oil, alongside a salad of preserved lemon, olives and fennel.

A recurring pleasure is discovering great wines where few think to look. Craven Wines captures that idea beautifully. It is proof that quality often lives off the fashionable paths, waiting patiently for someone curious enough to notice.

Jeanine Craven, a South African, and Mick Craven, from Australia, met in 2007 while working a harvest in California. For the next few years they kept moving, learning their trade in places such as the Barossa Valley, before returning to Jeanine's native Stellenbosch to be close to her family. There, without fuss or grand designs, they settled down and began making wines of their own.

Stellenbosch was not the obvious choice at the time. Much of the excitement in South African wine was gathering in the Swartland. Yet the town, only a short drive from Cape Town, has a long and noble history of viticulture. When the Cravens began searching for grapes for their own wines, they found something unexpected: a wealth of old vineyards that had fallen out of fashion and were suddenly available to those willing to look closely. It was the kind of serendipity that helped a young winery define its identity early on.

'Karibib' comes from a parcel of old bush-vine Chenin Blanc rooted in granite, its fruit long sold anonymously for the production of sweet wine. When the farmer died and his son took over, rather than keep sending the grapes to the co-op, he offered them to the Cravens, who reimagined the site as a high-quality dry wine.

In the warmth of Stellenbosch, the Cravens have shown a particular skill for crafting wines of moderate alcohol that deliver flavour and texture. 'Karibib' is a beautifully judged white, with notes of lemon, lanolin, white flowers, peach and a faint lick of salt. It is rounded, fresh, restrained, and all the more appealing for its price.

33

Domaine des Croix Beaune
A Town Built for Drinking

Region
Burgundy, France

Grape
Pinot Noir

Price
●●●○○

ABV
13%

Food
Serve this Beaune with roast chicken, mushrooms sautéed in butter and a green salad.

Next spread David Croix, Beaune

One of the rewards of being a Burgundy importer is returning, time and again, to Beaune – the beating heart of the region's trade. Anchored by the slender spire of the Hospices de Beaune and wrapped in a maze of bistros and bars, it's a place where drinking well isn't just encouraged – it's inevitable. Beaune can seem so devoted to pleasure – so intoxicated by its own conviviality – that it's easy to forget it is also a major appellation in its own right. In fact, only Meursault and Gevrey-Chambertin can claim a greater vineyard area.

Many years ago, wines from Beaune's 'Les Grèves' commanded the same respect – and the same price – as a kingly Chambertin. Beaune's standing later slipped down Burgundy's hierarchy, not through any failure of its soils, but because so much of its vineyard land remained in the hands of the large merchant houses, whose polished cuvées once defined the region's trade. As the 20th century unfolded, small growers across the Côte d'Or, long content to sell their fruit, began making and bottling their own wines, giving individual parcels an unmistakably personal voice. Beaune, still identified with the *négociant*, found itself out of step – too commercial, too workaday, for Burgundy's emerging cult of the grower-*vigneron*.

Beaune spent so long out of fashion that it never quite developed a fixed image in the minds of drinkers. In its own way, that absence has proved a blessing, creating space for small growers to take advantage of its off-trend – and therefore more accessible – vineyards. Beaune remains a commune capable of surprise, a reminder of how much pleasure Burgundy can still offer once you step away from the most exalted names. No one has done more to show what it can be – far beyond the fruity, easy-drinking style it became known for – than David Croix at Domaine des Croix.

Like his friend Sylvain Pataille up in Marsannay, David Croix has redefined what's possible in his hometown. His Beaune Premiers Crus – nearly two-thirds of the appellation holds that status – have become benchmarks, ranging from the delicate lacework of 'Les Grèves' to the dense, muscular drive of 'Pertuisots'. Yet for all the finesse and longevity of Croix's top wines, it's his straight Beaune that you return to most often. Year after year, it delivers: a vivid, unvarnished Pinot Noir that reminds you why this commune matters.

34

Dalamára Naoussa
The Greek Wine Revolution Is Already Here

Region
Macedonia, Greece

Grape
Xinomavro

Price
●●○○○

ABV
13%

Food
A plate of moussaka, or grilled Greek sausages (*loukanika*), would do nicely.

Some wines are rare. And then some wines are mythical. Dalamára 'Vieilles Vignes' ('old vines') Xinomavro belongs firmly in the latter camp. Produced in microscopic quantities – barely 600 bottles a year – this Greek red surfaces so infrequently that it has never had the chance to attain full-blown 'cult wine' status. But for those lucky enough to have found a bottle, it remains a benchmark – evidence that Greek winemaking can reach heights most people never imagined. Stylistically, it could be described as Macedonia's answer to Barolo, layered with notes of olive, dried tomato and herbs, alongside black cherries and balsamic, all carried by Xinomavro's dusty tannins. The perfume is so beguiling you might have to lash yourself to a mast, Odysseus-style, to resist.

In true mythical-wine fashion, no one seems sure whether the rumours of 'Vieilles Vignes' being discontinued are true. There is, however, some comfort in imagining its intense, old-vine fruit slipping into Dalamára's more accessible flagship, 'Paliokalias', and in knowing that the estate's entry-level Naoussa provides an inviting path into Greece's noblest red grape. Biodynamically farmed by sixth-generation *vigneron* Kostis Dalamaras, the Xinomavro here is handled with a Burgundian-like sensibility – which is where he trained. While his ancestors played a pivotal role in securing Naoussa's status as Greece's first appellation in 1971, today the family's solar-powered winery has emerged as a new reference point for the country.

To understand just how far Greek fine wine has come over the past 15 years, Dalamára Naoussa is an ideal place to start.

35

Below Chablis vineyards, northern Burgundy

Region
Burgundy, France

Grape
Chardonnay

Price
●●●●○

ABV
13%

Food
Oysters – always oysters; Dover sole in butter sauce; all kinds of mushrooms; and fudgy, soft cheeses such as Chaource and Saint-Marcellin.

Vincent Dauvissat Chablis

The Town That Thrives Against All Odds

No grape has been more lazily dismissed than Chardonnay. I don't mean the billions of overripe, heavily oaked, industrially processed Chardonnays that helped make it the most widely planted white grape on Earth – and sparked that '90s ABC ('Anything But Chardonnay') hate campaign, so successful that people still parrot it today. No, I mean the real thing: the raw material behind France's pre-eminent whites – from Montrachet and Meursault to the Côte Chalonnaise, the Mâconnais, Champagne, Jura and, on many days, my favourite of all, Chablis. Wines so incisive that most drinkers don't even realise they're drinking Chardonnay.

I've got a soft spot for Chablis, I really do. When it's made in the traditional way – raised in old oak barrels rather than exclusively in stainless-steel tanks – I can't resist its briny, oyster-shell aromas, evocative of sea air after rain. The finest cuvées age into something special: a mushroomy, lactic, Brie-like perfume, and a fine, chalky texture unlike anything else. It's a wine that could only come from this one place – and we're lucky it exists at all, because its survival has never been guaranteed.

Chablis is a handsome, faintly melancholic town in northern Burgundy, built from pale limestone and surrounded by wide, open plains. On 15 June 1940, during the Battle of France, the town had fewer than 1,800 inhabitants – making its bombing by the Luftwaffe all the more surprising. The attack came during the chaotic final days before France's surrender, as retreating French forces and advancing German troops clashed across Burgundy, and small towns like Chablis found themselves directly in the path of the fighting.

Many of the old timbered buildings in the town's medieval heart were reduced to ashes – centuries of history erased in a matter of hours. Miraculously, while the town burned, the vineyards – including the Grands Crus and Premiers Crus clustered together on a slope just to the north – escaped untouched. After the war, Chablis's winemakers rebuilt and carried on. Yet the challenges did not stop: in the 1950s, as many as one harvest in three was severely damaged or destroyed by another great enemy: spring frost. That Chablis not only survived but went on to thrive – becoming one of the world's defining white wines – feels almost miraculous.

When the wines are on form, there is a case for Vincent Dauvissat making the greatest Chablis of all – his real rival being Domaine Raveneau, located metres away on the same street. Years ago, I stumbled upon one of the

great buys of my life: a case of 2007 Dauvissat 'Les Preuses' Grand Cru, scandalously underpriced at a Notting Hill wine shop. Every bottle unfolded with cinematic, three-dimensional clarity before my astonished eyes.

These days, I drink Vincent Dauvissat whenever I can. In youth, they're electric – all cut glass and ocean spray – before tightening and falling silent for a while. Give them a decade, and they return in full technicolour glory. Occasionally, you find a bottle that's drifted into sherried territory – the heartbreak of premature oxidation – but more often than not, you find grace. Stick to the village Chablis and you'll rarely be disappointed; it's the kind of wine that reminds you why you fell in love with wine in the first place.

Below Vincent Dauvissat, Chablis

36-37

DOURO VALLEY
From Muscle to Charme

Niepoort 'Charme'

Region
Douro Valley, Portugal

Grapes
Red field blend

Price
●●●●○

ABV
13.5%

Luís Seabra 'Xisto Cru' Branco

Region
Douro Valley, Portugal

Grapes
Rabigato, Códega, Gouveio, Viosinho, Donzelinho Branco

Price
●●●○○

ABV
12.5–13.5%

Food
'Charme' makes me think of a pork chop with something earthy alongside – mushrooms or a bowl of lentils. 'Xisto Cru' calls for the sea: clams steamed with garlic and parsley, and plenty of bread to soak up the broth.

Left Luís Pedro Cândido da Silva, Niepoort, Douro Valley

Late on Christmas Eve 1997, after the pub, I opened a bottle of Niepoort vintage port. I knew nothing of the house or the Douro. It was Christmas, I was young, and there seemed no reason to stop pouring. The next day I conducted a private seminar on overindulgence from beneath the bedsheets. I've never been one to lose an entire day to excess, but this time the sun crossed the sky without me. Lunch passed. So did the afternoon. I had mistaken sweetness for mercy. The port – all velvet and holiday cheer – had concealed its authority. I can still taste it: dried fig, spirit, consequence. And, if I'm honest, the mild shame of disappointing my parents and grandmother, who had expected rather more animation from me that Christmas Day.

As my interest in wine deepened, I never quite moved beyond my yuletide faux pas. Out of step with the fashionable vinous styles of the years that followed, even the Douro's new wave of unfortified table wines struck me as overly alcoholic and lacking freshness – more muscle than grace. But the first sip of Niepoort 'Charme' showed how out of date that view had become. It freed me from my self-inflicted prejudice and revealed how deftly growers draw on fractured schist soils, varied microclimates and indigenous grapes to produce wines of lift and energy, shaped by the steep terraces of the Douro.

Luís Pedro Cândido da Silva, the 30-something winemaker who runs Niepoort's day-to-day operations alongside Daniel Niepoort, has a habit of disarming summaries. "There are no cool years in the Douro," he tells me. "Only less hot ones." It is not a joke. The region's climate is unforgiving: dry, sun-baked and extreme. In 2022, more rain fell in parts of the Sahara than in the Douro Valley. Vineyards here do not merely ripen; they endure. And yet Cândido da Silva also describes it as "Disneyland for winemakers" – not because it is frivolous, but because its dramatic shifts in altitude, exposure, soil and grape variety allow for an extraordinary range of styles.

Left Luís Seabra, Douro Valley

There are over 100 grape varieties planted together here as field blends. Over time they synchronise, adapting to the specifics of their site. The great port houses control vast tracts of vineyard, long producing wine at scale. But alongside them a different Douro has emerged: smaller, estate-bottled and increasingly precise. Dirk Niepoort, Daniel's father, has been central to the rise of unfortified wines in the valley. Taking over the family port house in the 1980s, he pushed it beyond its fortified heritage, championing dry Douro wines when few believed the region capable of finesse. While many producers pursued a Bordeaux template, prioritising extraction and new oak *barriques*, he sought an approach closer to the Côte d'Or wines he loved, placing less emphasis on deep colour, tannin and structure. That philosophy finds its clearest expression in 'Charme', a wine whose very name nods to Burgundy.

'Charme' has evolved over the years. The 2005 was rich and robust; the 2012 brighter, red-fruited. By 2018 it had grown more delicate – strawberries, a meaty undertow, a transparency through the fruit. But the 2022 vintage marked a decisive shift. Vineyard selection tightened, underperforming barrels were discarded, and the cellar cleaned and recalibrated. The summer was brutal – the hottest and driest since records began in 1934, with vines straining against heat intent on erasing nuance. And yet it produced an extraordinary 'Museu dos Lagares', a very pale, single-vineyard wine from the site that usually feeds 'Charme' – far finer and more ethereal than the Douro I thought I knew.

The Douro today feels less like a region chasing an external model and more like one discovering its equilibrium. Luís Seabra, Niepoort's head winemaker before Cândido da Silva, embodies another facet of that evolution. He left the company in 2012 to start his own project, part of a region newly confident in its voice. The Douro may be harsh, but it is not monolithic. It contains altitude and exposure, schist and granite – hillsides that yield both restraint and generosity. Alongside vibrant reds, the Douro also produces whites of steely tension, including Seabra's 'Xisto Cru' from high-altitude vines. A natural raconteur, he speaks of wine in terms of pleasure and place, not technicalities. "I'm famous for being last at the party," he says, laughing, "and for opening the most bottles." Yet beneath the conviviality lies seriousness: a belief that wine should sit naturally at the table, integrated into life rather than elevated above it.

SOUVEN

38

Domaine Dureuil-Janthial Rully
Away from the Cellar

Region
Burgundy, France

Grape
Chardonnay

Price
●●●○○

ABV
13.5%

Food
With the Rully Blanc, a simple *sole meunière* is hard to beat – as is a slice of warm Comté tart.

When I'm away on holiday – cut loose from my cellar, familiar restaurants and trusted wine shops – I revert to my natural state: just another customer, thirsty for value. I'm not in pursuit of Grands Crus. I'm looking for something humbler, more essential: wines meant to be drunk. Bottles that can be opened easily, poured generously and shared without that faint unease that something better ought to have been saved. They should be affordable enough to drink at lunch and again at dinner, yet deliver more than their price suggests. Above all, they should speak clearly of where they come from – and leave the day better than they found it.

In French wine shops, certain visual cues trigger a small, involuntary thrill. One of them is a yellow wax capsule crowning a bottle dressed in a plain livery of beige, white and blue – so unassuming it becomes almost conspicuously anonymous. Domaine Dureuil-Janthial wears its indifference to fashion proudly; whatever it lacks in aesthetic ambition is amply compensated for in the glass. These are wines that offer pleasure without pretence or a prohibitive price tag, tasting distinctly of their patch of the Côte Chalonnaise, of thoughtful farming and of a grower more concerned with precision than polish. They're the sort of Burgundies that remind you why Burgundy matters in the first place – not as a status symbol, but as a source of gastronomic joy.

Making arrangements to visit Vincent Dureuil at his Rully winery takes some doing – he spends most of the year working 14-hour days in his vineyards, bent on making the best bottles he can. As he pours his range of wines in the cellar, he is friendly and open, though with the sense that his real attention lies elsewhere. His reds and whites are arguably the finest in the whole of the Côte Chalonnaise, outshining many in the upmarket Crus of Chassagne-Montrachet and Meursault a few miles to the north. On holiday – and, in truth, at home – Dureuil-Janthial is what I drink.

39-42

ENGLAND
Britain's Not Faking It Any More

Domaine Hugo 'Hugo' Single Vineyard

Region
Wiltshire, England

Grapes
Pinot Noir, Pinot Meunier, Pinot Gris, Chardonnay

Price
●●●●○

ABV
11.5%

Daniel and Nicola Ham 'Many Moons'

Region
Essex, England

Grapes
Pinot Blanc, Chardonnay

Price
●●●○○

ABV
12%

Food
Lunch with these two bottles might begin with trout pâté and thickly buttered toast, then move on to *porchetta* with fennel and pomegranate salad.

Before you plant a vineyard, you should have a clear idea of what kind of wine you want to achieve. For most English sparkling producers, the target was clear: to replicate the *Grandes Marques* of Champagne, with as much gloss as possible. Domaine Hugo, though, didn't get that memo. Closer in spirit to Champagne's grower movement – where thoughtful farming matters more than polish – its sparkling wines have a distinctly English accent.

Wiltshire's climate doesn't make biodynamic farming easy – which helps explain why so few producers elsewhere in England attempt it. Having established a small estate in the Languedoc on biodynamic principles in 2003, Hugo Stewart brought those lessons home in 2016, planting Pinot Meunier, Pinot Noir, Pinot Gris, Pinot Blanc and Chardonnay on his family's farm in Cranborne Chase. In doing so, he set in motion one of the country's most promising new wineries.

Sheep graze among the vines in Domaine Hugo's chalk-soiled vineyards – an expression of the estate's philosophy, helping to build the conditions for more characterful fruit. Looking for a winemaker, Stewart wisely turned to Daniel Ham – now regarded, alongside his wife, Nicola, as one of the country's finest. In the farm's winery, Ham works with assured restraint, favouring wild fermentations, amphora ageing and no added sulphur – a demanding approach in a damp, unpredictable climate. The result is a singular, single-vineyard fizz: poised and expressive, with a depth that can disarm the staunchest English sceptic.

When it comes to still wine, Daniel and Nicola Ham's own domaine shows a clarity of intent that's rare on our shores. 'Many Moons', a tiny-production white made from fruit grown in Essex's Crouch Valley, has become a cult favourite thanks to its striking individuality. As Ellie Burt, sommelier at Noble Rot Mayfair, puts it: "'Many Moons' stands apart from England's sea of wannabe Burgundy – it's a brilliant bottle to pour blind if you want to challenge ideas about what England can do."

Langham 'Culver Classic Cuvée'

Region
Dorset, England

Grapes
Pinot Noir, Pinot Meunier, Chardonnay

Price
●●○○○

ABV
12%

Yarn 'Classic Cuvée'

Region
Dorset, England

Grapes
Chardonnay, Pinot Noir

Price
●●●●○

ABV

Food
Langham and Yarn are both perfect with oysters, langoustine and crab, simply prepared.

I'm sometimes asked what the future holds for English wine. I don't pretend to know the answer. But I do know what I've tasted. I remember the blind tastings we organised for *Noble Rot* magazine, when English sparkling wines were poured alongside Champagne, with no labels on view. In 2015 they won outright; in 2020 they came within a hair's breadth once again. But really, you don't need competitions or results to understand what's happening. If I'm asked the same question while in one of our restaurants, I could answer it by pouring a glass of Langham's 'Culver Classic Cuvée'. This Dorset-grown non-vintage fizz captures so much of what this sainted isle is capable of.

'Culver Classic Cuvée' is one of Noble Rot's by-the-glass mainstays, prized for the richness and harmony it delivers at its price point, and for how easily it complements our modern British cooking. That it has also become a go-to after-service drink for our sommeliers says plenty. If anyone can be trusted to spot genuine value among the hundreds of bins on our lists, it's them. Grown on chalky soils just outside Dorchester and vinified by Tommy Grimshaw, Langham's head winemaker, 'Culver Classic Cuvée' has fine, light-golden bubbles, layered notes of nuts, lemon and green apple, and a finely judged, saline finish.

Tommy Grimshaw is steadily establishing himself as one of England's most exciting winemakers. The debut of Yarn – a side project with his friend Alessandro Fraquelli, assistant winemaker at Jim Barry Wines – has only sharpened that impression. Working each year with pristine fruit from a single grower and limiting production to a few hundred bottles, the 2020 Yarn 'Classic Cuvée' set a new benchmark for what English sparkling wine can be in one of the warmest vintages that the country has ever had. With a nod to the oxidative style of Jacques Selosse, this is a broad, rich fizz, made with low dosage and deliberately reduced pressure, blurring the line between sparkling and still fine wine. I can't wait to see what comes next.

43

Equipo Navazos 'I Think' Amontillado
Who Gets to Drink the Good Stuff?

Region
Montilla-Moriles, Spain

Grape
Pedro Ximénez

Price
●●○○○

ABV
16.5%

Food
Makes everything from oysters and sushi to tandoori lamb chops shine a little bit more.

One of the awkward truths about fine wine culture is how hard it is to drink the very best bottles. With art, at least, anyone can walk into the Louvre and stand in front of the *Mona Lisa*, regardless of what they earn. Wine doesn't work that way. Very few people ever get to taste La Tâche. Yet by looking beyond today's most fetishised regions to once-fashionable places such as Jerez, most of us can still drink wines of real depth and pedigree in a kaleidoscope of styles. Equipo Navazos is one of the clearest proofs that this is still possible.

Back in 2005, Jesús Barquín, a wine-loving academic, and Eduardo Ojeda, a seasoned Jerez *vigneron*, began seeking out forgotten barrels in the dark corners of old *bodegas*. They took the name Equipo Navazos with no intention of going commercial. But after uncovering a remarkable solera in Sanlúcar de Barrameda, they gathered a few fellow obsessives, bottled Miguel Sánchez Ayala 'La Bota de Amontillado Nº1', and shared it among themselves. I'm fortunate to count one of that group as a friend, and at a dinner in Madrid he opened this inaugural Equipo Navazos bottling – revealing a bone-dry Sherry of remarkable finesse.

Over the years, I've enjoyed many of the duo's subsequent releases from what has matured into the regular 'La Bota' series. In that time, Equipo Navazos has evolved into a professional outfit – and while each release remains a limited bottling drawn from a rescued solera cask of venerable age, it has also begun making wines of its own, not least 'I Think' Amontillado.

If you can find more flavour, more complexity or more straight-up joy for the money than Equipo Navazos 'I Think' Amontillado, I want a glass. Although not technically a Sherry, as it comes from DO Montilla-Moriles, further inland than Jerez, this unfortified, 18-year-old Pedro Ximénez lifts the palate with layers of salted caramel, toasted walnuts, candied citrus peel and dried fruits. Equally at home at the beginning of a meal or at the end, it has a way of winning over those who might once never have given the classic styles of southern Spain a thought.

44

Thierry Fournier Champagne Réserve NV
Drink People and Places, Not Brands

Region
Champagne, France

Grapes
Pinot Meunier, Chardonnay, Pinot Noir

Price
●●●○○

ABV
12%

Food
Champagne is made for salt and crunch. Buttermilk fried chicken. Why the hell not?

'Champagne on a budget' is one of those phrases that usually signals impending disappointment. Too often it means a bottle stripped of character, with acidity running amok. The kind of fizz that has turned countless drinkers into lifelong sceptics, and rightly so. But now and then, if you're willing to dig past the industrial brands, you find something else entirely: a Champagne made by a farmer, not a factory. One grown by someone who actually drinks their own wine. For a restaurateur, finding such a bottle – one you can pour by the glass with pride – is a triumph. Thierry Fournier Champagne Réserve NV is exactly that sort of discovery.

There was a time, not so long ago, when Champagne seemed more concerned with image than with wine. Marketing departments polished the myth while the vineyards themselves were being strip-mined. Herbicides were widespread, and the land was even 'fertilised' with refuse carted in from Paris – an arrangement that seemed ingenious until plastic became unavoidable and toothbrushes began poking up between the vines. It was a chemically battered landscape, jarringly out of sync with Champagne's manicured reputation for luxury. Then a few clear-eyed growers began asking an unfashionable question: what if the wine tasted of something again? Figures such as Pierre Larmandier and Anselme Selosse chose another way. Herbicides were abandoned, yields cut and ploughs returned to the vineyards. It was valiant, against-the-grain work, running counter to the prevailing wisdom of the region.

'Grower' Champagne means that the person who makes the wine is the same person who farms the vines. While some also buy in fruit, it's the antithesis of the big houses, which blend grapes from hundreds of sources across the region to smooth away difference. As the reputations of the best *vignerons* have grown, so have their prices, but a younger generation is stepping into family estates with the same curious spirit. What was once an insider's secret has become some of the most compelling wine being made today.

Thierry Fournier is based in the Vallée de la Marne, the home of Pinot Meunier. Long treated as a supporting act – useful for flesh and fruit, but rarely trusted with the lead – Meunier has in the past two decades shown the heights it can reach when taken seriously, thanks to growers such as Jérôme Prévost. In Fournier's Réserve NV, it speaks clearly and with confidence. A generous proportion of reserve wines adds depth, while extended time on the lees gives extra dimension. The result is a richer, more rounded texture, layered with notes of nougat and lemon cream.

GEWURZ-TRAMINER
1946
GRAND VIN

45-46

GEWÜRZTRAMINER
The Pleasure of Being Wrong

Pierre Weber '3 Orange' Gewürztraminer

Region
Alsace, France

Grape
Gewürztraminer

Price
●●○○○

ABV
12–12.5%

Marcel Deiss Gewürztraminer

Region
Alsace, France

Grape
Gewürztraminer

Price
●●○○○

ABV
14%

Food
Gewürztraminer is great with exotic spice, but its true calling is Munster cheese – preferably so ripe it's crawling off the plate.

A wise man once said that anyone in pursuit of self-improvement should be content to appear clueless. God only knows how many times I've clung to that mantra while blind-tasting at Vantre, Marco Pelletier's *bistrot à vins* in Paris's 11th, often feeling like an actor sweating through the pause before their first cue. Pelletier, the outspoken former head sommelier of Taillevent, possesses a command of fine wine that makes most so-called 'masters' look like enthusiastic interns. When I dine here, I never see a label until the glass is drained and the interrogation complete. His cellar may groan with coveted names, but woe betide the "fucking trophy hunters" who dare to request them outright. No, the surest way to engage Pelletier is to ask for something cold, wet and alcoholic that he loves... and that you almost certainly don't yet know.

Where else but at Vantre could you stumble upon venerable yet modestly priced Pouilly-Fuissés, Savennières and Chinons made by long-forgotten *vignerons*? Or a rare Savoie Chasselas, aged under flor like a yellow wine – one of countless treasures here that prize individuality over sterile consistency? Soulful bottles such as these remind us that price and luxury have never been synonymous. What matters is not what a bottle costs, but how it makes you feel. And yet, on a casual drop-in, fresh from the TGV at Gare de Lyon, Pelletier poured me one of the most humbling glasses of my life.

Introduced as a 'singular' pairing for Indonesian-spiced turbot, the mystery wine glows in my glass, bright yet hazy, like sunlight through antique amber. It is unmistakably an 'orange' wine, slipping nimbly between spice and heat, coaxing harmony from flavours that might otherwise clash. I lift the glass and catch wafts of lychee and rose petals – fresh, alive, memory flooding back in an instant. On the

Above Marco Pelletier,
Vantre, Paris

palate it isn't showy or overwrought, but poised. A fine layer of tannins gently grips the sides of the mouth, and the finish lingers.

"What do you think?" Pelletier asks.

I trust my first instinct. "Gewürztraminer – maybe from one of Alsace's new-school winemakers experimenting with extended skin contact. Someone like Mathieu Deiss."

He studies me with the stillness of a poker player guarding a royal flush. "And the vintage?"

With the vagueness born of too many wrong guesses, I hazard: "Around six years old."

"You're right, it's Gewürztraminer – but a little older."

From behind a folded napkin, he produces an Alsace flute: slender, pale green, the words 'Clos Zisser' glinting on its yellow label. My eyes lift to the neck label: 1946.

The dining room seems to fall silent. It feels like being slipped a Montrachet when all I'd ordered was a house wine.

1946 Louis Klipfel 'Clos Zisser'. A 79-year-old Gewürztraminer from part of Alsace's Grand Cru 'Kirchberg de Barr' – a reminder of why this off-trend region has vineyards with Grand Cru status. In that pre-technological era, Gewürztraminer's pink berries would have been pressed for far longer than is usual now, with extended skin contact lending the wine its amber glow. If surprise is what fuels fascination with wine, this bottle goes nose to nose with the greats. Gewürztraminer – gloriously incapable of being anything but its flamboyant self – is one of the easiest grapes to pick blind; it might as well sashay in wearing sequins. Yet here, amid the perfume and swagger, it carries me back to Christie's Wine Course in Fitzrovia in the mid-2000s, to that first wide-eyed sip.

For those starting to explore wine, Gewürztraminer's heady perfume offers an easy thrill to cling to – though later it is often dismissed as lacking seriousness. Many write it off as blowsy: full-bodied, high in alcohol, with acidity scarcely worth the name; others find its brazen personality impossible at the table. And yet, when it's right – ripeness balanced by freshness – it dazzles. Indonesian spices sing with it. Foie gras purrs. Even a Munster so pungent it could floor a horse preens into a beauty queen beneath its gaze.

I can't begin to suggest where you might track down a bottle of 1946 Louis Klipfel 'Clos Zisser'. But Pierre Weber '3 Orange' Gewürztraminer, from high-altitude Husseren-les-Châteaux, is one of the most characterful modern versions I've drunk since. Bright orange-pink, with a subtle prickle of volatile acidity to lift its mandarin and apricot fruit, it finishes bone-dry with a delicate, bitter-amaro edge.

Gewürztraminer often needs food to bring out its best side and, like 'Clos Zisser' with Indonesian fish, I'll never forget being served it with ripe Munster for the first time at Domaine Weinbach – a combination that transcended either element alone. That same harmony can be found with the lush, spice-laden Marcel Deiss Gewürztraminer – an alchemy that makes wine feel surprising all over again.

47

Giaconda Estate Vineyard Chardonnay
On Struck Match

Region
Beechworth, Victoria, Australia

Grape
Chardonnay

Price
●●●●●

ABV
13–14%

Food
Wood-grilled lobster or black cod brushed with miso would be sublime.

Right Giaconda vineyards, Victoria

Next spread Rick Kinzbrunner, Giaconda

At a time when Australian winemaking errs on the side of caution, Giaconda Chardonnay stands apart – a classic forged through its refusal to follow fashion. It has become a benchmark for Australian Chardonnay, with recent vintages hailed as among the finest the country has produced – all the more remarkable within a culture that still venerates the new over the classical.

Planted in the early 1980s by Rick Kinzbrunner – who once worked at Napa's legendary Stag's Leap – Giaconda Chardonnay owes its distinctive, smoky-reductive character to a combination of the vineyard's soils and extended lees ageing in oak. "I've always loved those old white Burgundies with their matchstick perfume," says Rick, now working alongside his son Nathan. "We're not trying to imitate Burgundy, but getting close isn't necessarily a bad thing."

Tasting with Rick and Nathan in Giaconda's Beechworth cellar is a thrilling experience. While some barrels are smokier than others, all share that unmistakable struck-match fragrance, balanced by Chardonnay's gentle, creamy-lemon richness. Less confident winemakers might try to clean it up, worried drinkers will see it as a fault.

Giaconda's wines have remained consistently brilliant, with freshness, depth and length that bear out the Kinzbrunners' convictions. These days they pick earlier, as many do in Australia, to preserve freshness – a far cry from the heavy, overripe styles that once drove drinkers to declare, "anything but Chardonnay".

The origins of struck-match aromas in wine are far from an exact science – even Burgundian domaines famed for them admit they don't fully understand why some vintages show them and others do not. Known as 'reduction', a product of low-oxygen winemaking, it walks a delicate line – taken too far, it can yield sulphurous notes of rubber, rather than the flinty precision that marks the best examples. In France's Jura, Stéphane Tissot makes exceptional single-vineyard Chardonnays, often serving them blind to show how their character is shaped by soil. From limestone, the wines are racy and linear; from clay, broader and deeper, with a struck-match perfume absent from the limestone.

48

Château Gloria
Class Without Classification

Region
Bordeaux, France

Grapes
Cabernet Sauvignon, Merlot, Cabernet Franc, Petit Verdot

Price
●●○○○

ABV
14%

Food
A pan-fried rib of beef with Yorkshire pudding, gravy and horseradish sauce.

Bordeaux has a weakness for hierarchy. It clings to its sacred 1855 classification, a ranking of châteaux into five growths, the way someone grips a crumbling ledge. Never mind that a century and a half has passed, that the climate has shifted, techniques have evolved and the way people interact with fine wine has changed. If you're not in the 1855 hierarchy, forget it – you're background noise.

Naturally, one of the most interesting figures in Bordeaux over the last century was someone who didn't care about any of that. Henri Martin wasn't born into a First Growth château. He didn't have a title, a trust fund or a vineyard handed to him because his great-great-grandfather once poured wine for Napoleon III. What he had was entrepreneurial drive and good taste.

Martin had spent years helping to steward the vineyards at Château Latour through great vintages like 1982. He could've stayed there forever, but he wanted his own estate. So he did the unthinkable. He began buying tiny slices of precious Saint-Julien vineyards from the grand old châteaux around him – vineyards no one ever planned to part with, except by inheritance.

Parcel by parcel, he assembled a patchwork of golden terroir: from Léoville-Poyferré, from Gruaud Larose, from Ducru-Beaucaillou. He called it Château Gloria, after his wife. And then he had the nerve to make wines that rivalled the classified growths – without the comforting stamp of 1855 approval.

Was it heresy? Oh yes. Is it delicious? Abso-bloody-lutely.

Today, Gloria represents the Médoc without the pomposity, and unlike many of the classed growths – whose recent releases are now, crazily, often more expensive than their fully mature vintages – it remains a steal. Elegant and refined, it frequently performs better than wines at three times the price in my pal Stephen Browett's annual Southwold Group tasting, where a Bordeaux vintage is reviewed blind by critics and merchants. It's the kind of wine you can buy by the case: drink a few bottles now over long Sunday lunches, and watch the rest develop over time.

Henri Martin proved that in Bordeaux, the land of rules, rankings and reverence, you could still build something great with your own two hands and aim a middle finger squarely at out-of-date tradition. And that, frankly, is glorious.

49

Guilhem & Jean-Hugues Goisot 'Exogyra Virgula' Sauvignon de Saint-Bris

The Only Appellation in Burgundy Permitted to Produce Sauvignon Blanc

Region
Burgundy, France

Grape
Sauvignon Blanc

Price
●●○○○

ABV
13%

Food
Oysters; goat's cheese (Crottin de Chavignol, Sainte-Maure, Ragstone); seafood tartare.

Plenty of people have it in for Sauvignon Blanc, and I can't pretend they're entirely wrong. This is, after all, the grape that gave rise to the comparison of 'cat pee'. In the wrong hands, it can be loud and aggressively green – more lawn clippings than vineyard. The worst New Zealand examples hit you with a chemical blast of gooseberries before settling into something unmistakably feral – as though a tomcat has just marked his favourite wall. Much of what passes for Sancerre today seems more interested in broadcasting pedigree than expressing place. You could call it prestige inflation, with branding racing ahead of taste.

But in the right hands – say, those of Guilhem Goisot, working in the out-of-the-way Saint-Bris at Burgundy's northern edge – it becomes something else: honest, characterful and exceptional value. Saint-Bris AOC sits near Chablis, within the Auxerrois cluster of appellations, also including Irancy, Chitry and the Côtes d'Auxerre. Uniquely, it is the only appellation in Burgundy authorised to produce Sauvignon Blanc and Sauvignon Gris, rather than Chardonnay or Aligoté. That singularity makes Saint-Bris a regional outlier – less an anomaly than a survivor of older traditions.

'Exogyra Virgula' Sauvignon de Saint-Bris is far more restrained than its New Zealand contemporaries, with a subtly saline, Chablis-like austerity born of similar Kimmeridgian limestone soils. ('Exogyra Virgula' refers to the tiny fossilised oysters found here.) In truth, Domaine Goisot ought to sit comfortably among the fine estates of Chablis. When phylloxera ravaged the region in the late 19th century, however, appellation boundaries were redrawn, and Saint-Bris found itself pushed out of the Chablis fold. A pity, because the connection is obvious the moment you set foot in the vineyards.

Farmed biodynamically, this Sauvignon de Saint-Bris shares many of the virtues of the best Sancerre – and none of its detractors' dreaded cat pee. It's the kind of bottle that demonstrates that wine culture is less a straight line than a patchwork of historical quirks.

50

Domaine Pierre Gonon Saint-Joseph Rouge

A Perfume That Defies Expectation

Region
Northern Rhône Valley, France

Grape
Syrah

Price
●●●●○

ABV
13%

Food
Serve it with a roasted leg of lamb, scented with rosemary and garlic. The wine's pepper and olive notes speak the same dialect as the dish.

Right Jean Gonon, Domaine Pierre Gonon, Mauves

I've always believed it's better to follow people, not reviews – producers rather than vintages or appellations – to listen to how they think, watch how they farm and pay attention to how they make their wine. That, more than anything, is the surest way to find wines that speak to you. And if you ever come across the name Domaine Pierre Gonon on a bottle, don't hesitate for a second – buy it. The Gonon brothers simply don't put a foot wrong.

Saint-Joseph Rouge sits at the heart of Jean and Pierre Gonon's domaine. I've lost track of how many bottles I've drunk over the years, but every glass reminds me why it's such a treasure. In a world where egos and prices rise far faster than vines could ever grow, this cuvée has remained grounded. It carries that unmistakable Gonon perfume: violets, black pepper, smoke and the subtle hum of well-hung game. Few wines express their place, and their makers, with such steady conviction.

Like anyone farming grapes on the steep, terraced hillsides of Saint-Joseph, where every inch of work is done by hand, the Gonons are *vignerons* in the truest sense. Down on the flatter ground of Crozes-Hermitage, a single grower can look after as much as 15ha with the help of machines and irrigation; here, one person is lucky to tend a single hectare. Saint-Joseph is a sprawling appellation – its vineyards stretch for nearly 50km along the banks of the Rhône – and the name on the label alone is no guarantee of quality.

Saint-Joseph AOC was founded in 1956, anchored around five granite valleys – Les Chalaix, Bachasson, Sainte-Épine, La Dardouille and Saint-Joseph itself. Expansion, however, has done it few favours. From some 600ha in the early '90s to more than 1,400 today, Saint-Joseph has pushed outward, adding roughly 30ha a year, as if growth itself were a virtue. The best slopes can rival Côte-Rôtie or Cornas, but too often producers have planted vines where it's easiest, not where the finest grapes are grown.

And then there are Jean and Pierre Gonon. Since their father Pierre Gonon's day, they've transformed the family domaine from a supplier of easy-drinking wines for local bistros into a producer whose bottles command the attention of sommeliers everywhere. Their wines have that evocative perfume and sinew that remind you what Saint-Joseph once promised – and what, in the right hands, it still can be.

51

Doniene Gorrondona 'Iri'
The Wine You Pour from Above Your Head

Region
Basque Country, Spain

Grape
Hondarrabi Zuri

Price
●○○○○

ABV
12–12.5%

Food
'Iri' is in its element with *pintxos*, the Basque Country's answer to tapas – small, flavour-packed bites such as *gildas*, *foie à la plancha*, and grilled scallops and prawns.

Left Txakoli vineyards, Getaria, Basque Country

If you love great food and wine – and if you're reading this, you almost certainly do – and you haven't been to San Sebastián, clear your calendar and go. This Basque city will unfold before you like a well-laid table: plates of glistening anchovies, thick-cut *txuleta* rib steak and endless pours of cool, briny Txakoli. Pronounced 'cha-ko-LEE', Txakoli is a session-style wine that is performatively served in San Sebastián's *pintxo* bars, with bartenders raising bottles above their heads and pouring into a glass held far below, a ritual that releases trapped CO_2 and gives the wine its natural spritz. Also made as less-popular sparkling, red and rosé styles, much Txakoli is cheap and industrially produced, with little to recommend it beyond moderate alcohol and clean, crisp, citrus-and-green-apple flavours. Yet it is too easy to write it off as one-dimensional, especially while pioneering producers such as Doniene Gorrondona approach its production with the rigour required of a fine wine.

Winemaking in the Basque Country stretches back 1,500 years. A century ago, taverns known as *chacolines* – which served Txakoli alongside seafood – were popular in San Sebastián and nearby towns such as Getaria, pairing the wine's saline freshness with traditional fish delicacies such as gelatinous cod cheeks (*kokotxas*), goose barnacles (*percebes*) and baby eels (elvers). The high rainfall and persistent humidity in the region make grape-growing difficult, and over the course of the 20th century, swathes of Txakoli vineyards disappeared as labourers moved to cities in search of easier work.

In 1989, a small group of producers halted Txakoli's slide towards oblivion by helping to establish its first quality-minded appellation, DO Getariako Txakolina, followed by DO Bizkaiko Txakolina and DO Arabako Txakolina. Each DO permits a different mix of varieties, though the wines are built around the region's signature grapes – Hondarrabi Zuri and Hondarrabi Beltza – supplemented by historic local varieties and, in some cases, international grapes. Doniene Gorrondona 'Iri' is a crisp and harmonious white from Bizkaiko Txakolina, with real body and richness, that operates on similar frequencies to a good Vinho Verde or Muscadet Cru. Txakoli like this expresses a deeply rooted culture – one that rewards exploration.

52

Domaine Gour de Chaulé Gigondas '.1871 Les Jardinières'

Rethinking Gigondas

Region
Southern Rhône Valley, France

Grapes
Grenache, Syrah, Cinsault, Counoise, Carignan, Mourvèdre

Price
●●●○○

ABV
14–14.5%

Food
Daube provençale meets 'Les Jardinières' on garrigue-strewn ground.

Gigondas isn't exactly a name that sets wine lists alight these days. Many people have written off this storied Provençal village as the land of boozy, sunburnt reds from another era – the sort of thing liable to get you cancelled in a Paris wine bar. But even the most unfashionable appellations have their treasures. Look past the clichés and you'll find producers like Domaine Gour de Chaulé, a centuries-old estate now in the hands of 20-something Paul Fumoso, crafting authentic wines of real character and freshness.

'Les Jardinières' Gigondas is no shrinking violet – nor should it be. Yet through excellent farming and careful whole-cluster fermentations, Fumoso achieves that elusive balance of muscle and finesse, running counter to Gigondas's reputation. Wine has been made in this idyllic part of the southern Rhône since Roman times, when it housed a convalescent camp for legionaries. The name Gigondas comes from the Latin *jucundus*, meaning 'delightful' – a fitting tribute to its landscape of Aleppo pine forests and, two millennia on, to Fumoso's wines.

Gigondas is often compared to Châteauneuf-du-Pape, though their terroirs could hardly be more distinct. Both appeal to lovers of full-bodied reds, but where Châteauneuf tends towards breadth and force, Gigondas is typically brighter and more lifted. Curious and driven, Fumoso continues to refine his approach, looking beyond the region to learn from leading *vignerons*. The result is a small range of ambitious Grenache-based wines, carrying their richness with ease. Given an hour or so in the decanter, his cuvée 'Les Jardinières' opens to aromas of strawberry and baking spice, with warm stone and liquorice. Where many Gigondas tip into overripe fruit and excess alcohol, this is an old-school beauty, handled with restraint.

53

Below Ramiro Ibáñez, Sanlúcar de Barrameda

Region
Sanlúcar de Barrameda, Spain

Grape
Palomino

Price
●●○○○

ABV
10.5–12%

Food
Tuna carpaccio with olive oil and lemon zest, or *spaghetti alla bottarga*.

Bodegas Ramiro Ibáñez 'UBE de Ubérrima Miraflores' *Sherry, Reimagined*

Spain's white wines are among the most compelling in the world, and few make the case more persuasively than Ramiro Ibáñez's unfortified Palomino, 'Miraflores'. Long defined by Sherry – a wine shaped as much by blending and fortification as by place – Palomino here takes a different path. Ibáñez bottles individual *pagos* such as UBE 'Miraflores' and allows them to speak with clarity and conviction. Released by vintage rather than drawn from a solera, these wines belong to the tradition of Vinos de Pasto (table wines): saline, Atlantic-edged whites informed by biological ageing, yet anchored in the vineyard.

Grown in Sanlúcar de Barrameda's chalky *albariza* soils, 'Miraflores' is aged in old Sherry *botas* beneath a delicate veil of flor, yielding Manzanilla-like notes of almond, yeast and sea spray. Such flavours can challenge the uninitiated, but here they are subtle and precise – perfectly attuned to contemporary tastes for freshness and moderate alcohol. Alongside the unfortified Palominos he produces with Willy Pérez as De la Riva, and those of friends such as Alejandro Muchada (of Muchada-Léclapart), Ibáñez's wines are natural partners for seafood. They show that Palomino can be every bit as noble – and as eloquent an expression of place – as the finest French varieties.

54

Domaine Corinne, Jean-Paul, Fanny & Loïc Jamet Côte-Rôtie

Smells Too Good to Be Just Grapes

Region
Northern Rhône Valley, France

Grape
Syrah

Price
●●●●●

ABV
14%

Food
Roast grouse and bread sauce with Domaine Jamet Côte-Rôtie would be near the top of my last-supper list. A charred rib of beef is not far behind.

Right Loïc, Jean-Paul and Fanny Jamet, Côte-Rôtie

Next spread Côte-Rôtie slopes

Trying to arrange a meeting with a winemaker in Côte-Rôtie by email is like sending smoke signals into a mistral – they vanish into the ether, carrying your hopeful message to who knows where. But really, can you blame them? If your daily commute involved hauling yourself up a vertigo-inducing hillside of ancient stone terraces so sunburnt it's literally named the 'roasted slope', you might not be glued to Outlook either. Take Loïc Jamet of the venerable Domaine Jamet: at 5.30 a.m. in mid-July, he's already zipped into full hazmat gear, spraying vines that cling to the slopes like survivors. By 8 a.m., while some of us are still negotiating with our snooze buttons, the heat is closing in and the work is done. This kind of grape-growing demands more than just dedication. It requires a quasi-religious belief so consuming that even the most persistent inbox doesn't stand a chance.

The obvious question is why anyone would grow grapes on such vertiginous slopes when the flatlands – where you can drive a tractor without risking an obituary in *Viticulture Monthly* – are so much easier. Masochism may play a role, but the answer is invariably in the wine. At its best, Côte-Rôtie offers one of wine's most entrancing perfumes: an otherworldly reverie quite unlike anything else. Other Northern Rhône appellations that specialise in Syrah come stylistically close. But line them up blind and Côte-Rôtie nearly always gives itself away, announcing itself with a flourish of violet and rose aromas intertwining with berries, sap, smoke and game. And speaking of game, when asked that well-worn 'ultimate wine-and-food pairing', nothing beats Domaine Jamet Côte-Rôtie and roast grouse, the savoury Syrah echoing the bird's wild, iron-rich flavours.

Jamet

Previous pages Loïc Jamet, Domaine Jamet cellars

Below Dan Keeling and Loïc Jamet, Fongeant vineyard, Côte-Rôtie

No matter how often I drink Jamet Côte-Rôtie, it always smells too good to be just grapes. Of course, I know it's not just *any* grapes, but what remains hard to believe is that back in the 1950s Côte-Rôtie was difficult to sell. With apricots fetching three times the price of Syrah, many *vignerons* abandoned the slopes to grow fruit on the plains. At that time, Côte-Rôtie was a cheap wine served in local bars, surviving postwar labour shortages only thanks to the rise of chemical fertilisers and herbicides. By the 1960s, when the government compulsorily bought vineyards on the flatlands to construct the Paris-Marseille *autoroute*, growers turned their attention back to the terraces. In the 1970s, *vignerons* such as Marius Gentaz and Albert Dervieux built reputations on deeply individual wines made much as their forebears had done. But it was the Ampuis *négociant* Marcel Guigal who truly changed Côte-Rôtie's fortunes, his 'La Mouline', 'La Landonne' and 'La Turque' single-vineyard bottlings propelling the appellation onto the global stage.

Domaine Jamet may bottle a single-vineyard Côte Brune, but it remains convinced that the strength of Côte-Rôtie lies in the blend: young and old vines from across the slopes, brought together in harmony. It has also always stayed true to the tradition of fermenting whole bunches of grapes, stems included – a practice that lends the wines their sappy, herbal freshness and creates an instantly recognisable thread. "My father, Jean-Paul, always believed in the soils," Loïc Jamet, who has taken over the running of the domaine with his sister Fanny, tells me. "When he first started, people were dismissive of his use of whole bunches, calling it 'the old way'."

Once tasted, Jamet Côte-Rôtie needs no further explanation; you quickly see why people have been coming back, year after year. Perhaps it's how it feels at once untamed and reassuring, with something of Burgundy's fragrance and Bordeaux's structure. Or perhaps it's that moment when the wine's roasted perfume takes flight – a visceral swirl of violets, olives, cloves and well-hung game that stills conversation. There are many reasons why Jamet's Côte-Rôtie endures. You need only taste it.

Mas Jullien
PAYS D'HERAULT
2016
MIS EN BOUTEILLE AU MAS
Mas Jullien
2018
Mas Jullien

55

Mas Jullien Terrasses du Larzac 'Autour de Jonquières'
They Say Quality Never Goes Out of Style. It Does

Region
Languedoc-Roussillon, France

Grapes
Mourvèdre, Carignan, Syrah

Price
●●●●○

ABV
13.5%

Food
Good with lamb – shoulder, neck, or chop – cooked slowly or grilled simply.

Next spread Olivier Jullien, Languedoc

Wine goes in and out of fashion, like everything else. In the 1980s it was the turn of the Languedoc – that sprawling, sunburnt corner of southern France, long dismissed as *vin ordinaire* – to suggest something more. Mas de Daumas Gassac made the case first, planting Cabernet Sauvignon and other non-native varieties where no one had thought to look, and proving that a *grand vin* could come from unassuming soils. Its success prised the door open for a new generation. Grange des Pères, Mas Jullien and others followed, guided less by fashion than by conviction – the belief that great wine need not come from a blue-blooded château.

Attention has moved on, and the Languedoc has slipped back towards its old reputation for industrial wine. Yet Mas Jullien kept its own course. Its owner, Olivier Jullien, remained on his rocky terraces at the foot of Mont Saint-Baudille, drawing whites and reds from land that first found wider recognition thanks to its austere beauty. A meticulous farmer, Jullien spent years trading and replanting parcels until the estate felt entirely his own. The vineyards are among the highest and most exactingly kept in the south of France, where cool nights and stony soils preserve freshness and balance.

Jullien remains devoted to native grapes – Carignan, Cinsault, Grenache, Syrah and Mourvèdre among them. I've loved drinking his vibrant, garrigue-scented cuvées on holiday in the south of France, and, just as much, plush yet still-fresh bottles of 'Autour de Jonquières' from the 1990s. A couple were once poured blind by his former UK importer Roy Richards. Richards also represented estates such as Le Pin and Armand Rousseau, yet years later still held these wines in such high esteem – which says much about their maker.

56-58

JURA REDS
The Twilight Zone of Red Wine

Bénédicte & Stéphane Tissot Arbois 'DD'

Region
Jura, France

Grapes
Ploussard, Trousseau, Pinot Noir

Price
●●○○○

ABV
12–14%

Cellier Saint Benoît Arbois Pupillin Ploussard 'La Ronde'

Region
Jura, France

Grape
Ploussard

Price
●●●●○

ABV
12–13.5%

Food
Ploussard's light body and gentle earthiness make it ideal when served slightly chilled alongside roast chicken with morels.

Here we go with the tired tropes: "The first duty of wine is to be red." It's a cliché so outdated you can almost hear it creak, yet it still helps explain why top-end red wines command higher premiums than whites. These days, though, if you're one of those bloodthirsty imbibers who deride whites as palate-cleansers, ask yourself what the first duty of a red wine really should be. Twenty-five years ago, 'serious' wine lovers described oaky, opaque Cru Classé Bordeaux as the blueprint. Since then, Burgundian Pinot Noir has seduced the world, and sensibilities have changed. The young reds I adore are fresher, paler and more moderate in both tannin and alcohol – from dark 'rosés' such as Cerasuolo d'Abruzzo to sensual Ploussards made by Jura growers such as Stéphane Tissot, Cellier Saint Benoît and Houillon-Overnoy. Ploussard (also known as Poulsard outside of Pupillin, the Jura village that claims the variety as its own) is a singular grape whose characteristics inhabit the space between where *vin blanc* ends and *vin rouge* begins. It's the twilight zone of red wine.

Jura is historically known as a white wine region, located a mere Vacherin's throw from the Swiss border. Here, locals consider their white – and famous yellow – wines the main event, while native red Ploussards and Trousseaus are the warm-up acts, often served as aperitifs (I know – perverts). Just a decade ago, growers were struggling to sell their red wines. Now, Ploussard and Trousseau are as fashionable as it gets. What makes them so compelling is that the best could only ever come from this one place on the planet. Ploussard, in particular, is an uncommonly delicate red that exists in a register of its own. If you were to drink a glass without seeing its colour, you could easily mistake it for a white. Its naturally thin skins account for hues of pale red, pink or orange. Indeed, Stéphane Tissot recalls customers once complimenting him on his "rosé" during a period when

Emmanuel Houillon-Pierre Overnoy Arbois Pupillin Ploussard

Region
Jura, France

Grape
Ploussard

Price
●●●●●

ABV
12.5%

Ploussard was out of favour, even though his single-varietal cuvées and the delicious 'DD' – a blend that also includes Trousseau and Pinot Noir – are anything but insubstantial.

Judging the quality of a wine by its depth of colour is rather like judging a sentence by its length. Winemakers are taught in school to extract as much colour as possible, but Ploussard rewards a gentler hand. My first experience of the grape was Domaine Houillon-Overnoy's legendary cuvée. Brilliant pale pink and perfumed with pomegranates, rose petals, white pepper and lychees, it felt like a bottle that had fallen out of the back of a spaceship – wildly exotic yet reassuringly wholesome. Now semi-retired, Pierre Overnoy is the closest the Jura comes to vinous royalty, with his protégé, Emmanuel Houillon, at the helm of their Pupillin winery – the self-proclaimed Capital of Ploussard, perched in the hills above Arbois. Traded at punishing premiums, Houillon-Overnoy's improbably coloured Ploussards have become the reference point.

Just up the road in Pupillin, Cellier Saint Benoît is run by Benjamin Benoît, a young grower who has begun to establish himself in recent vintages. Raised in the village but shaped by time in Burgundy, he returned to make single-vineyard Ploussards that speak of place rather than easy, glou-glou drinking. "When I returned from Burgundy, where the focus was on the character of individual plots, I asked, 'Why don't we do that here?'" says Benoît. Today, he practises regenerative farming and bottles five distinct Ploussard Crus that are as precise as they are pleasurable.

Page 148 Benjamin Benoît, Cellier Saint Benoît, Jura

Left Ploussard – the twilight zone of red wine

59-60

WEINGUT KELLER
A German Estate with a Cosmopolitan Palate

'Von der Fels' Riesling

Region
Rheinhessen, Germany

Grape
Riesling

Price
●●●○○

ABV
12–12.5%

Food
'Von der Fels' Riesling suits herb-driven Vietnamese dishes or simply seasoned tempura.

'Talfels' Chardonnay

Region
Rheinhessen, Germany

Grape
Chardonnay

Price
●●●●○

ABV
13%

Food
'Talfels' is at its best with caramelised scallops or a prawn cocktail.

The Keller family have dismantled many assumptions about Rheinhessen wine, listening closely to their vineyards while measuring themselves against Europe's greatest wines. Husband and wife Klaus-Peter and Julia Keller have always looked beyond borders, finding points of reference from Burgundy to the Mosel – not as models to copy, so much as conversations to join. The resulting Grosses Gewächs Rieslings are powerful, razor-cut and unapologetically dry, with a stony persistence that carries on long after the glass is empty – the kind of wines they love to drink themselves. Yet the appeal of this Flörsheim-Dalsheim estate doesn't stop at the top. There's real pleasure to be had in 'Von der Fels', an entry-level Riesling that delivers more than it suggests, and a sense too that the estate isn't standing still – as son Felix and his wife, Bella, push further into new territory with Chardonnay.

'Von der Fels' Riesling Trocken shows how much pleasure a great estate can deliver before prestige ever enters the conversation. Drawn from younger vines and more modest parcels, it nonetheless carries that unmistakable Keller clarity. *Trocken* means dry, and this wine takes that promise seriously. It shares the same discipline and intent found in the estate's top bottlings, albeit with a little less weight and nuance, at a gentler price. Notes of citrus peel, fresh herbs and smoke sit atop a firm mineral spine. Given time, 'Von der Fels' settles into something even deeper and more complex.

'Talfels' is a different wine, and the Burgundy-shaped bottle it comes in offers a telling clue. A Chardonnay counterpart to 'Von der Fels', made from young vines in the Kellers' best parcels, it points to a growing trend among younger *vignerons* who relish the freedom of working outside an established Riesling rulebook. Not long ago, Chardonnay wasn't legal in Germany, and where it was planted it rarely ripened. Today, Rheinhessen's climate feels closer to Burgundy's a few decades ago, a shift that, alongside similarly limestone-rich soils, makes the grape an obvious choice.

Making something distinctive from the world's most widely planted white grape is a challenge. Yet with Burgundians such as Olivier Lamy providing inspiration – the Kellers have adopted his high-density planting to achieve old-vine levels of concentration – it's little surprise that 'Talfels' already ranks among Germany's most compelling new wines. The chiselled first release from 2023 reveals a citrus-and-gunflint perfume with impressive density and persistence. Less an experiment than a statement, it's a debut worth following closely.

61

Peter Jakob Kühn 'Quarzit' Riesling Trocken
For People Who Think They Don't Like German Riesling

Region
Rheingau, Germany

Grape
Riesling

Price
●●○○○

ABV
11.5–12.5%

Food
Grilled asparagus, simply dressed with lemon, olive oil and salt – a notoriously tricky pairing – works beautifully.

People who claim they don't like German Riesling are usually protesting against sugar or excess, not the grape itself. Peter Jakob Kühn indulges neither: no sweetness, no potpourri perfume – just the steely authority of a wine that knows what it wants to be. 'Quarzit' Riesling Trocken has a dryness and verve rarely expected of the category. Lime skin, wet stone and a savoury grip define it – more architectural than aromatic.

Kühn sits in the front ranks of dry German Riesling alongside masters such as Rheinhessen's Klaus-Peter Keller and the Mosel's Clemens Busch. Based in the Rheingau, he has spent years refining his farming and winemaking, drawing on wild yeast fermentations, long lees ageing and occasional skin-contact macerations, inspired in part by winemakers such as the late Stanko Radikon. After a serious illness in his family, he adopted biodynamic methods to promote healthier soils, aiming for Rieslings of tension and elegance rather than the ubiquitous fruity style.

Up until the mid-1990s, producing dry Riesling in the Rheingau was a struggle. Grapes rarely ripened enough to reach 12% ABV, and the resulting wines were thin and marked by shrill acidity. As the climate warmed, longer growing seasons allowed Kühn to produce more complete dry wines. Since 2018, the estate has been led by his son, Peter Bernhard Kühn, who has introduced refinements while remaining faithful to the family's ethos. They continue to be clear expressions of vintage and vineyard, shaped more by savouriness and spice than fruit. 'Quarzit' Riesling Trocken is an intense, linear introduction to the style, with the Crus gaining flesh and breadth through to Kühn's summit, the stony and resonant 'Schlehdorn'.

62-63

LANGHE NEBBIOLO
The Most Over-Performing Red Wine Appellation in the World

Azienda Agricola Giuseppe Rinaldi Langhe Nebbiolo

Region
Piedmont, Italy

Grape
Nebbiolo

Price
●●●●○

ABV
14–14.5%

Ca' di Press Langhe Nebbiolo

Region
Piedmont, Italy

Grape
Nebbiolo

Price
●●●○○

ABV
14%

Food
More versatile than its big brother Barolo, Langhe Nebbiolo pairs well with everything from terrines and salami to pizzas, pastas and roasts.

Left Carlotta and Marta Rinaldi, Azienda Agricola Giuseppe Rinaldi, Barolo

Next spread Barolo town

The best bottle on the table is usually the one that's empty first. Not the most expensive, not the one everyone talked about beforehand, but the one that's drained while others are barely touched. Piedmont, despite its reputation for grandeur, understands this better than most regions. If you're hunting for trophies, it won't make things difficult: there are plenty of shops where the most magnificent Barolos are displayed like relics, handled with museum-style care. Yet, of late, some of the most compelling wines there aren't Barolo at all, but Langhe Nebbiolo – the supposedly lesser appellation beneath it. Unencumbered by such strict controls on how it must be aged, many of these wines have an energy and approachability better suited to the way we drink today.

Whether you're shopping in Piedmont or Pimlico, it's easy to assume the more expensive the bottle, the more pleasure it will provide. It often doesn't. The true luxury lies in a wine that feels right from the first sip to the last – and, happily, such moments have never been the sole preserve of the priciest Crus. And so, even as Barolo grows more famous than ever before, some of the most exciting developments in Piedmont are unfolding in the category below. Long regarded as its cheaper sibling, Langhe Nebbiolo is increasingly seen as a serious wine, more reflective of individual philosophies in the vineyard and cellar, and offering a clear expression of the region today.

It's intriguing that the Italians, often thought of as more anarchic than the regulation-worshipping French, whose winemaking innovations they've long adopted, have bound their own *vignerons* with stricter rules. Chief among them are controls governing how long, and in which vessels, wines must be aged: from the onerous requirements of Brunello di Montalcino (60 months before release, including a minimum of 24 months in oak) to the more moderate Barolo (38 months, with at least 18 months in oak). Set against Burgundy – so often wheeled out as Piedmont's closest stylistic cousin – where winemakers enjoy near-total freedom over *élevage* (to the extent of abandoning oak entirely in favour of ceramic tanks, or whatever else takes their fancy), such controls feel distinctly prescriptive.

In practice, Nebbiolo's formidable acidity and tannins are well served by long, traditional ageing in large oak *botti*. The porous staves let the wine breathe, taming the

Left Alice Pressenda, Ca' di Press, Perno, Monforte d'Alba

tannins and building complexity. Since Barolo must spend a minimum of 18 months in oak – a requirement that inevitably enforces a degree of stylistic homogeneity – several growers I spoke to expressed frustration at their inability to shorten this period in difficult vintages, such as 2024, when many wines lacked the concentration to withstand prolonged ageing in wood. By contrast, Langhe Nebbiolo is made to suit the fruit, not the regulations.

Langhe Nebbiolo is Nebbiolo unshackled: fruit drawn from across the Langhe's mist-covered, rolling hills, from lesser-known communes to young vines within Barolo and Barbaresco. It often comes from small parcels in otherwise prestigious sites, the bits edged out of the DOCG by altitude or exposure. For generations, such hierarchies were grounded in a simple truth: some sites ripened reliably; others did not. Today, as warmer seasons carry even the humblest sites to full maturity, those old divisions are beginning to blur. A vineyard need not have a famous name to yield a wine of real beauty when handled with care.

The level of seriousness accorded to Langhe Nebbiolo varies widely. Many growers continue to treat it as a simple varietal wine. Others, like sisters Carlotta and Marta Rinaldi at Azienda Agricola Giuseppe Rinaldi, instead make a Langhe Nebbiolo of real ambition that drinks like a lighter, more digestible Barolo, its perfume of black cherry and undergrowth carried on fine, supple tannins. That should come as little surprise once you know the wine draws on less-favoured parcels in their lofty Bussia and Ravera Crus, and is raised for a full 18 months in large oak *botti*, followed by a further two months in bottle before release. "I drink Langhe Nebbiolo more often than Barolo," says Carlotta Rinaldi. "I'm curious to taste other producers' cuvées, because I see it as their calling card – a clear expression of their style."

I've been impressed by both this so-called 'baby Barolo' school of winemaking and a more lightly handled style that lets the fruit do the talking. Even at its most generous, Nebbiolo remains a demanding grape, especially for newcomers more accustomed to soft tannins and challenging flavours. In that context, brighter, fruit-led expressions can feel like a friendlier way in. "I don't like Langhe Nebbiolo that tastes like Barolo – I prefer it fresh and easy to drink," says Alice Pressenda of Ca' di Press. Her approach takes shape in the spring following the harvest, when she sets aside tanks of the most complex young wines for oak ageing and eventual release as Barolo. The remaining lots stay in stainless steel for nine months, followed by a year in bottle, before being released as Langhe Nebbiolo.

Ca' di Press make a wine for real life: a bottle you're as happy to open on a Tuesday night with a takeaway as you are sharing around a crowded table of friends. But with both lighter and more serious styles this far apart, it's fair to ask what, if anything, Langhe Nebbiolo stands for. The answer, as ever in Italy, is that its strength lies in its refusal to behave.

64

López de Heredia Rioja 'Viña Gravonia' Crianza Blanco
The Value of Refusal

Region
Rioja, Spain

Grape
Viura

Price
●●○○○

ABV
12–13%

Food
Viña Gravonia Crianza Blanco is at its best with Marcona almonds, *jamón ibérico*, paella, mushroom rice and anchovies.

The best definition of a brand I've heard is that it's the most valuable real estate in the world – a corner of someone's mind. For me, one of those corners has long belonged to Bodegas López de Heredia. Its ancient cellars, buried beneath the town of Haro in Rioja, are a kind of ordered madness: a maze of cobwebbed chambers housing traditional, long-aged wines that feel less made than unearthed. I've been carrying this place around in my head for years, and I'm content for it to stay there.

Tasting with owner María José López de Heredia is also to understand that a brand is defined as much by what it refuses to do as by what it does. I've drunk López de Heredia wines dating back to the 1930s that remain astonishingly fresh and alive, and I'm in awe of how they have stayed true to themselves when so many of their neighbours were seduced by technology and gave up what had once made them distinctive. On my last visit, María José opened a 1970 'Viña Tondonia' Gran Reserva Blanco, its perfume bursting with candied orange peel and a saline lick of sea urchin, underscoring how vital it has been for it to preserve the methods that give rise to such long-lived greatness.

Those old bottles are not easy to come by. But López de Heredia's current releases are still among the great values in wine. 'Viña Gravonia' Crianza Blanco comes from Viura grown in the Gravonia vineyard, just outside Haro. It doesn't rush it. The wine spends about four years in old barrels, then six or more years in bottle before it's released – a long wait for a white, and one that makes perfect sense when you taste it. The long ageing gives 'Viña Gravonia' its deep golden colour and that mix of nutty, honeyed flavours that comes with a touch of oxidation – very much old-school Rioja, and very much its own thing. No matter what else I'm drinking, I always find my way back to it.

Right López de Heredia Viña Tondonia cellars, Haro

Next spread Stocks of López de Heredia wines

Left María José López de Heredia, Haro

65

Domaine Luneau-Papin Folle Blanche
A Civilised Way to Drink Less

Region
Loire Valley, France

Grape
Folle Blanche

Price
●○○○○

ABV
11%

Food
Oysters, clams, cockles, mussels – Folle Blanche is made for shellfish.

Look, if you don't drink, that's fine. Good for you. But let's stop pretending the booming No-Lo category has anything meaningful to do with real wine. Wine is about risk, fermentation, taste and storytelling – good conversations and ideas. It is not a brand stripping alcohol out of industrially farmed, flavourless grape juice and flogging it back with a whiff of sanctimony and a generic label. If you're avoiding alcohol, drink a delicious tea – or, radical thought, a glass of water. Still undefeated. But if you're cutting back and want flavour, culture and pleasure without the lie, there are exceptional moderate-alcohol wines that deliver all of that honestly.

At 11% ABV, Domaine Luneau-Papin's Folle Blanche is ideal for those wanting a wine with lunch that won't go to their head – and, crucially, doesn't require you to suspend disbelief along with your buzz. There is a huge contrast between this and a 15% ABV bruiser from a warmer climate – both during and after. Many 1980s Cru Classé Bordeaux come in at 12–12.5% ABV, rather than the 14–14.5% now commonplace – the difference between getting on with your day and losing the afternoon entirely.

Domaine Luneau-Papin sits in Le Landreau, near Nantes, and has, over time, helped reposition Muscadet as a serious, terroir-specific wine. But whereas Muscadet is made from Melon de Bourgogne, this Folle Blanche is bottled within the Gros Plant du Pays Nantais appellation and is another grape entirely – lighter-bodied, crisper, more electric. For today's restrained lunchtime drinking culture, it offers citrusy-saline refreshment at a low price – and authenticity.

66

Bodegas y Viñedos Rodrigo Méndez 'Cíes'
Spain, with a Chance of Rain

Region
Rias Baixas, Galicia, Spain

Grape
Albariño

Price
●●○○○

ABV
12–13.5%

Food
Octopus with olive oil, paprika and potatoes (*pulpo a la gallega*) is the most emblematic match. Calamari and seafood rice dishes suit it just as well.

In Val do Salnés, the Atlantic governs everything. In this old heart of Galicia's coastal white-wine country in Rías Baixas, the air is cool, rain frequent, and Albariño grows almost everywhere. It is one of northern Spain's great viticultural gifts and, paradoxically, one of its most taken-for-granted grapes. As many wineries in the region have drifted towards industrial uniformity, Rodrigo Méndez has stayed close to home, working patiently with old vines around Meaño. He treats Albariño as Burgundians treat Chardonnay: a grape capable of nuance, for those willing to listen.

In Méndez's hands, Albariño isn't flashy. It is chiselled and precise. Much of what passes for Albariño today tastes generic – engineered to be reliable, inoffensive, anonymous. From old vines and well-chosen sites in Val do Salnés, however, it is capable of something more exacting. It registers differences in soil, exposure and proximity to the sea with remarkable definition. Méndez works simply: native yeasts, old oak long abandoned elsewhere, no overt manipulation. Nothing is forced. The wines have composure – naturally high acidity lending lift and tension, with a depth of texture that sets them apart from the forgettable norm.

Méndez usually vinifies his vineyards separately – sometimes in more than 18 bottlings – but 'Cíes' is conceived differently: a blend of small parcels intended to give a clear picture of the place. The wine is straight and brisk, with firm acidity and a saline edge that reflects its Atlantic setting. It is comfortable with shellfish, poultry, even richer sauces, holding its line without asserting itself. This is not Albariño made to impress on its own. It is made to be drunk with food. Albariño on its own terms.

67

Château Montlandrie
Someone Actually Tried

Region
Bordeaux, France

Grapes
Merlot, Cabernet Franc, Cabernet Sauvignon

Price
●○○○○

ABV
13–14.5%

Food
Duck confit with lentils.

The world of wine is full of over- and underachievers. Bordeaux, in particular, has never lacked either. There are estates that inherited greatness and spent decades polishing it into something safe. Then there are people like the late Denis Durantou, who took a modest, largely overlooked patch of Pomerol at Château L'Église-Clinet and worked it into one of the most compelling wines on the Right Bank. While others chased scores, Durantou sought character: old vines, low yields and the stubborn belief that terroir mattered more than brand. The results weren't engineered to please everyone, only to represent the truth. When you're choosing what to drink, the question is simple: do you want a wine made by someone who coasted – or by a visionary like Durantou, who did the work?

That doesn't mean you have to spend hundreds on Durantou's revered Château L'Église-Clinet (though a great year – 2012, for example – will reward you with one of the finest Pomerols made). True to his tireless nature, he also bought other estates in less exalted corners, turning them into similarly overachieving wines – a legacy now carried on by his daughters, Noëmie and Constance. Château Montlandrie in the Castillon Côtes de Bordeaux – acquired in 2009 and extensively replanted – is a shining example. Set on a similarly south-west-facing limestone slope to the lauded Château Ausone – just a few miles away in Saint-Émilion – one taste of a strong vintage explains its regular success in critics' blind tastings, offering delicious early drinking and the structure to improve over time. With an elegant perfume of blackcurrant lozenge and spice leading to silky tannins, it's a red that feels almost implausible for the money.

68

Domaine Jacques-Frédéric Mugnier Chambolle-Musigny
A Certain Frequency

Region
Burgundy, France

Grape
Pinot Noir

Price
●●●●●

ABV
12.5–13%

Food
Quail braised with shallots, lardons, sage and peas – a trusty companion to great red Burgundy.

Right The Winery, Maida Vale, London

My pal David Motion owns London's most charming wine shop. Tucked away near the languid canals of Little Venice – a part of the city that resists the urge to hurry – The Winery is a small, beautifully proportioned room, preserved much as it was when it served as a pharmacy in the Victorian era. Dark wooden shelves, worn smooth by generations of use, line the space, and on chilly winter evenings a working fireplace offers a welcome glow. It's the sort of place where one can imagine Dickens stepping in to buy some claret and lingering by the hearth.

David's great passion is dry German Riesling, and his shelves hold the finest collection in the country. Yet curiosity – the essential companion of any true wine lover – draws him well beyond the Mosel. It was here, in The Winery, that I first encountered the Chambolle-Musigny of Jacques-Frédéric Mugnier, still a novice and armed mainly with enthusiasm. From that moment, Burgundy took hold.

Chambolle-Musigny is a small commune in the Côte de Nuits, long locked in a friendly rivalry with neighbouring Vosne-Romanée for the title of Burgundy's most mystical vineyards. I say mystical because there is no better word for the aura that hangs over the top Grand Crus of these two communes – Musigny on one side, Romanée-Conti on the other. At its core, wine is nothing more than fermented grape juice. Yet every so often, a bottle appears that makes that definition feel naïve.

The Grand Cru Musigny I eventually bought from David was one such wine. When I opened it a few days later, it seemed to vibrate at a different frequency from anything I'd tasted before. This wasn't a wine that sat politely in the glass. It seemed to levitate above it – intense, yes, but somehow weightless – smelling at once of summer flowers and of something faintly animal, something unmistakably alive.

Freddie – as he's affectionately known – makes barely five barrels of Musigny in a good year. It's a heartbreakingly small yield, priced well beyond what most people would ever dream of paying for a bottle of wine. A couple of rungs below that summit sits his village wine, Chambolle-Musigny, a more attainable window into the same silky register, drawn from parcels surrounding the Grand Cru. It is a red Burgundy that explains, in a single glass, why this corner of France became holy ground.

pH3,2

69

Família Nin-Ortiz 'Planetes de Nin' Carinyena Blanca
High Acidity, Low Oxygen

Region
Priorat, Spain

Grape
Carinyena Blanca

Price
●●○○○

ABV
13%

Food
Try this with *calçots* – those big, sweet spring onions you throw straight on the grill – with a light romesco sauce made of peppers, hazelnuts and olive oil. The char and sweetness bounce nicely off the wine's acidity, and the whole thing stays firmly Catalan.

Left Carles Ortiz, Família Nin-Ortiz, Priorat, Catalunya

It seems fitting that mountaineer-turned-*vigneron* Carles Ortiz, who has scaled El Capitan by three different routes, should now grow grapes on the vertiginous slopes of Priorat in Catalunya. Together with his wife, Ester Nin, he farms a small estate near the village of Porrera, where working the vines can feel less like agriculture than like climbing with a hoe. The couple belong to a new generation of *vignerons* here who pursue finesse through indigenous grape varieties, rather than the extracted, oak-laden international blockbusters that seized critics' attention in the 1990s. Both are, by their own admission, 'acid freaks' – obsessive in their pursuit of freshness in a region where heat and drought can easily tip fruit into overripeness. When I visited during harvest, they wore T-shirts emblazoned with 3.2 pH – the level of acidity they consider essential to making wines of clarity and poise, rather than sticky caricatures.

'Planetes de Nin' Carinyena Blanca tells you a lot about who Nin-Ortiz are. Carinyena Blanca is a grape that makes bureaucrats nervous because it doesn't rack up alcohol the way the rulebook prefers – but in the vineyard, and in the glass, it makes all the sense in the world. It's a variety built for drought, for heat, for poor soils, and it gives a wine that's stony and floral, carried by a line of acidity. In an era when climate change is rewriting the rules, this is exactly the kind of grape – and the kind of wine – we should be paying attention to. That it isn't recognised by the DOCa Priorat says more about the limitations of the system than the wine. Here, tradition isn't something frozen in time; it's something rediscovered, and the result is a wine that has a sense of place you can't fake.

70

Stéphane Ogier 'L'Ame Soeur'
The 2,000-Year Comeback

Region
Northern Rhône Valley, France

Grapes
Syrah, Viognier

Price
●●●○○

ABV
14%

Food
Game birds are a natural fit, but there's no need to feel bound to meat. This is just as good with ratatouille, or even a plate of well-charred vegetables.

Left Stéphane Ogier, Côte-Rôtie

Stéphane Ogier is one of the leading growers of Côte-Rôtie, those vertiginous slopes south of Lyon where Syrah finds its true voice – floral, olive-scented, smoky, and touched with fat and game. Since 2001, though, his curiosity has carried him across the Rhône to Seyssuel, a place sometimes called 'up-and-coming', though only if you ignore the fact that it began making wine some 2,000 years ago. The Romans knew these hills well; Pliny the Elder and Martial wrote about their wines with affection long before neglect allowed them to fade into obscurity. Today, the vineyards are alive again, and Seyssuel is once more yielding Syrah of striking perfume, fully capable of standing beside its more celebrated neighbour.

Seyssuel's renaissance began in the 1990s, when three Rhône veterans – Yves Cuilleron, Pierre Gaillard and François Villard – decided that the old Roman slopes deserved another chance. They replanted Syrah and Viognier on the vertiginous schist terraces and bottled their wines under the IGP Collines Rhodaniennes, while lobbying for an appellation of their own. Today, some 14 growers work these hillsides, still waiting for official AOC recognition, yet producing wines that hardly need it. Seyssuel is warmer than Côte-Rôtie, and the air carries the scent of garrigue; walk among the vines and it feels unmistakably as though the south has begun.

'L'Ame Sœur' – 'the soulmate' – is Stéphane Ogier's love letter to Seyssuel: a wine that carries much of Côte-Rôtie's grace and fragrance, but speaks in a slightly sunnier voice of its own. It sells for a bit less than his Côte-Rôtie, though it comes from equally demanding slopes and receives the same meticulous care. In the best years, it can stand alongside its more famous neighbour, and on occasion even steal the show. Aromatically, it's all roses and violets, followed by a savoury hint of bacon fat and spice, and a refreshing edge that reminds you how distinctive – and how difficult to imitate – Northern Rhône Syrah is.

71

Domaine de la Pépière Muscadet Sèvre et Maine Sur Lie 'Briords'

How Muscadet Got Its Dignity Back

Region
Loire Valley, France

Grapes
Melon de Bourgogne

Price
●●○○○

ABV
11.5–12%

Food
Don't overthink it. Give it something simple: oysters still dripping with brine, clams steamed and barely dressed, or a piece of white fish grilled over fire with nothing more than olive oil and a squeeze of lemon. The wine will do the rest.

Left A plate of Carlingford oysters and a glass of Domaine de la Pépière Muscadet Sèvre et Maine Sur Lie 'Briords'

Muscadet was once the go-to wine to drink with a plate of oysters by the sea – salty, fresh, crisp and honest. Then came the era of chemical farming and ramped-up yields, when costs mattered more than taste. Muscadet lost not only its character but its dignity, reduced to little more than the punchline of a bad joke. Yet the region has since begun to renew itself, focusing on organic farming and a lighter touch in the cellar. Domaine de la Pépière released its first single-vineyard cuvée, initially known as 'Clos des Briords', around the turn of the millennium – a wine that has become one of the leading lights of a revolution redefining Muscadet as one of France's classic whites.

Muscadet lies south-east of Nantes, on the windswept Atlantic coast. Made exclusively from the Melon de Bourgogne grape – tragically rechristened 'Melon B' – the best examples are strikingly pure and intense, with a salty finish reminiscent of Chablis, though that's largely where any resemblance ends. At its best, however, Muscadet offers a fine mineral clarity and restrained alcohol – qualities perfectly attuned to contemporary tastes.

Muscadet producers don't dig deep cellars. They can't – the water table's too high. Instead, they ferment and age their wines in large, glass-lined concrete tanks set into the floor. The young wines sit on their lees – the spent yeast that protects them from oxygen – and over time develop a depth and texture that surprises anyone who assumes Muscadet is merely a low-quality style. The term *sur lie* first appeared on Muscadet labels in 1977, intended as a signpost of quality. At the time, it mattered. Today, it mostly tells you that the wine was bottled in the year following the harvest – and not much else. Ironically, some of the most serious, long-aged Muscadets now fall outside the designation altogether. Labels, it seems, have a way of lagging behind reality.

'Briords' shows what Muscadet can be when it's treated with patience and respect, dismantling whatever prejudices linger from the region's industrial past. At this price, it's hard to think of another white wine that delivers so much character with such ease.

72

Pierre Péters Cuvée de Réserve Blanc de Blancs Grand Cru Brut
Cold Precision

Below The road to Le Mesnil-sur-Oger, Champagne

Next spread Le Mesnil-sur-Oger

I arrived late the first time I went to meet Rodolphe Péters. The Côte des Blancs was locked in winter – as it often seems to be when I'm in Champagne – and the road down into Le Mesnil-sur-Oger was like an unbroken sheet of ice. I barely brushed the brakes and the car started to slide sideways, the vines flashing past in slow motion. We crept the rest of the way like a horse on glass, arriving at Pierre Péters a full 40 minutes behind schedule. Rodolphe just laughed – the weather holds no surprises for him – and poured a line-up of wines that made the nerve-shredding drive feel worthwhile.

It's no coincidence, then, that Rodolphe – the sixth generation of the Péters family farming in Le Mesnil-sur-

Region
Champagne, France

Grapes
Chardonnay

Price
●●●○○

ABV
12%

Food
Linguine with clams and lemon zest – the wine's salinity mirrors the brininess of the clams.

Oger – describes the village's wines as 'wintry'. A specialist in finely wrought, crystalline Chardonnay, the commune is home to two of Champagne's most fabled cuvées – Krug's Clos du Mesnil and Salon. Yet Péters's comparatively modestly priced 'Les Chétillons' shares their chalky precision and singular sense of place, demanding years of bottle age to reach its potential. In the meantime, the house offers a range of more immediately accessible wines, beginning with Cuvée de Réserve Blanc de Blancs Grand Cru Brut.

Cuvée de Réserve is where the domaine's signature style – saline, chalky and pure – comes into focus. A blend of multiple vintages, often five or six years' worth, it is made from Chardonnay grown in Grand Cru villages of the Côte des Blancs. Pale gold, with a fine, persistent mousse, it has a bright core of what Rodolphe calls "cold stone and citrus". A gentle creaminess rounds out the palate, lending balance and finesse. It drinks like a Champagne twice the price: the definition of a house benchmark.

73

Phelan Farm 'Autrement'
A Man Who Chose Otherwise

Region
Cambria, California, USA

Grapes
Pinot Noir, Gamay, Mondeuse

Price
●●●●○

ABV
12.5%

Food
'Autrement's' freshness makes it a natural companion to poultry, especially roasted quail and pigeon.

It wasn't a Grand Cru or anything with a pedigree worth bragging about – just a humble country wine that ended up changing the course of Raj Parr's life. Parr – one of America's most gifted sommeliers, a restless taster and evangelist for the old ways of France – had spent much of his working life roaming vineyards, cellars and bistros. In Paris with friends, he found himself returning again and again to a modest *bar à vins* in the 13th arrondissement, La Fine Gueule, devoted to wines made without sulphur. There, night after night, they drank magnums of a fresh, nervy Savoie blend of Pinot Noir, Gamay and Mondeuse that refused to let them go: Jacques Maillet's 'Autrement'. And before Parr quite knew it, what began as curiosity became devotion – as if the wine were gently insisting on a different way forward.

Autrement is a French word that means 'otherwise', or 'in another way' – a modest name that nonetheless announced Jacques Maillet's early faith in biodynamic farming and natural winemaking, back when such convictions were still

viewed as eccentric, even reckless, in Savoie. The wine itself spoke just as plainly: lively acidity lifting aromas of Alpine herbs and red fruit, shaded by a faint, earthy note that recalled the cellar floor more than any laboratory. It was a simple, honestly made wine – and one that lodged itself in Parr's imagination.

Back in Santa Barbara months later, Parr received a call from a grower, Greg Phelan, who wondered if he might be interested in buying Chardonnay and Pinot Noir from vineyards he had planted in Cambria, San Luis Obispo County – a remote stretch of California scarcely associated with wine. Parr thought the fruit might suit Sandhi or Domaine de la Côte, two projects he was involved with at the time, and made the long drive north. Once there, the place suggested something else entirely. "As soon as I saw the vineyards," Parr recalls, "I knew it was a place where I could plant Gamay and Mondeuse and make the kind of wine I really want to make." Instead of buying grapes, he bought the entire estate. He gave up his itinerant life and moved there on his own in October 2020 – just as the world was closing down.

Phelan Farm is made up of three small vineyards encircled by forest, in a remote corner of California with scarcely 2,000 inhabitants – no paved roads, no reliable internet, and only a couple of wells for water. Parr arrived already questioning a life spent in perpetual motion, worn down by six years of sustained research for his second book *The Sommelier's Atlas of Taste*. He began planting and farming, guided more by instinct than instruction. Months passed in lockdown without his seeing another person. In that isolation, he grew more patient. With no consultant to call, questions had to be carried, turned over, and answered in their own time.

Parr set out to build an ecosystem, planting late-ripening varieties – Mondeuse, Savagnin, Gringet – that he had come to admire in France's quieter corners. In Cambria's cool climate, these grapes found the long, unhurried growing season they require. The wines that result are modest in alcohol, ranging from 11% to 12.5%, yet they carry a natural depth of flavour and a kind of unforced energy.

Over several vintages, and through the steady discipline of regenerative farming, Parr has clarified the voice of Phelan Farm. At first, he refused sulphur altogether, in the vineyard and at bottling, trusting the wines to find their own balance. With time, he came to see restraint as a form of care, and today he uses sulphur sparingly at both stages, giving the wines greater clarity and stability. In generous years he bottles several cuvées, shaped by grape and circumstance. But 'Autrement' – his own reading of Jacques Maillet's now-discontinued wine, made with permission and in a similar spirit – remains the estate's touchstone. Blended from the same three grapes, it offers red fruit, pepper and hints of oolong tea, lifted by a forest-born freshness and a salinity that recalls the nearby Pacific Ocean.

Left Raj Parr

74

Place of Changing Winds 'Heathcote Syrah'

In Search of an Australian Somewhere

Region
Heathcote, Victoria, Australia

Grape
Syrah

Price
●●●●○

ABV
13%

Food
Roasted duck with Chinese five spice, or smoky aubergine with tahini and herbs.

Not everyone in Australia believes greatness in wine comes from place. Penfolds Grange, the country's celebrated red, offers an example. Instead of coming from a single plot, commune or region, it is made from fruit sourced nationally. A remarkable wine, certainly, but also proof that, down under, terroir has not always served as the guiding principle. Part of the explanation lies in the separation of grape growing from winemaking. Most wineries rely on purchased fruit rather than growing it themselves and, as a result, exercise limited influence over farming. Can you hope to make world-class wine when its most important element is left largely in someone else's hands?

'Wine is made in the vineyard' may be a galumphing cliché, but Europe's biggest leaps forward have come from people returning to the vines. Countless elements must fall into place – the right plants in the right spot, cared for properly and picked at just the right moment – before anything exceptional can happen. Just as the Champagne grower movement drove a long-overdue return to serious farming, Australian winemakers, too, have begun to prioritise place over brand. Few embody that shift more clearly than Melbourne-based wine importer-turned-*vigneron* Robert Walters.

As the Australian agent for some of Burgundy's most innovative domaines, Walters has seen first-hand how improved farming can elevate a wine. At his Place of Changing Winds estate in the Macedon Ranges – a cool-climate area north of Melbourne – he too is now experimenting with high-density plantings that encourage competition between vines and deeper root systems, producing fewer but far more intensely flavoured grapes. Against a national average of roughly 2,000 vines per hectare, Walters's average of nearly 15,000 – rising to as many as 33,000 in some blocks – is testament to his ambition.

Australian single-vineyard wines are nothing new – Henschke Hill of Grace dates back to the 1860s. But by investing in cutting-edge farming and winemaking techniques gleaned from some of France's great growers, Walters is pursuing something more exacting than many of his contemporaries. Place of Changing Winds' 'Heathcote Syrah', sourced from a site on the Mount Camel Range rather than assembled from multiple vineyards, is a good introduction to his search for a new Australian sense of somewhereness. Dark, fresh and savoury, it shows how far a bit of stubborn idealism can go.

75

Bodegas Ponce 'Clos Lojen'
These Wines Mean Business

Region
Manchuela, Spain

Grape
Bobal

Price
●○○○○

ABV
12.5%

Food
Jamón serrano, sausage and fennel ragù, lentils with smoked paprika.

Ponce is part of a tiny, blessed fraternity of wineries whose names provoke a schoolyard chortle from the Anglophone brain. But make no mistake: the wines themselves are no joke. They're dead serious – pure, soulful and shaped by a master *vigneron* who doggedly applies exacting farming across Manchuela's slopes, transforming what was once an anonymous inland zone into one of Spain's most compelling high-altitude terroirs. Giggle at the name if you want to, but these bottles will shut you up real quick.

Juan Antonio Ponce (pronounced 'PON-thay') worked for Compañía de Vinos Telmo Rodríguez, gaining experience across some of the country's finest winemaking projects, before returning home to start his own. Manchuela is a high plateau of rolling vineyards, 600–900 metres above sea level, tucked between Valencia and La Mancha. For decades it served as a back-country source of Garnacha, Monastrell and the humble Bobal, most of it destined for bulk wine. While Garnacha and Monastrell enjoy established pedigrees elsewhere, Bobal long remained in the shadows – valued for yield rather than character. Only recently has it been allowed to speak for itself, and in Ponce's hands this once-modest grape proves it has far more to say than anyone imagined.

For all its affordability, Bodegas Ponce 'Clos Lojen' keeps company with far finer wines – it's simply better than it has any right to be. Farming 70ha of vines, Ponce has upended the local ethos by pursuing quality as well as quantity. For this cuvée, he whole-bunch ferments Bobal from 60-year-old organic vines in large, old oak vats, then matures the wine in *foudres* of various shapes and sizes.

'Clos Lojen' is fresh and expressive, with fragrant floral notes, gentle herbs and a supple finish. At a modest 12.5% ABV, it's not what you'd expect from a land-locked corner of central Spain. Ponce has rewritten Bobal's reputation, steering it away from the heavy, extracted reds of the past towards finesse and purity – and in the process delivering one of the great bargains in modern wine.

76

Le Ragnaie Rosso di Montalcino
Same Hills. Same Grape. Less Waiting

Region
Tuscany, Italy

Grape
Sangiovese

Price
●●○○○

ABV
13–14.5%

Food
Bistecca alla fiorentina with beans stewed with tomato and sage.

These pages are filled with *vignerons* who don't compromise. They give themselves to their *métier*, sustaining both land and family through good years and bad. I admire them for their passion and tenacity, without any illusion that I share their calling. Yet when I am sometimes asked where, of all the places I have visited, I would choose to make wine, my thoughts drift to Brunello di Montalcino in Tuscany: to bowls of *ribollita* and monumental cuts of *bistecca alla fiorentina*; to its timeless patchwork of vineyards, olive groves and cypress-lined ridges; and to Sangiovese, which, at its best, possesses a sensuality that few grapes can rival.

I fell in love with Brunello di Montalcino through the otherworldly reds of the late Gianfranco Soldera. But I cannot help but pity young producers setting out to make wine in this demanding appellation, which requires them to endure no fewer than five years of legally mandated ageing – at least two of them in oak – before they can sell their first bottle. It was for this reason that Rosso di Montalcino came into being. Made, like Brunello, from pure Sangiovese – sometimes from the same vineyards – it is spared the strictures of the law, requiring only that the wine rest for a minimum of ten months before release, in whatever vessel the grower deems fit.

For producers, Rosso di Montalcino provides a chance to stay solvent while the grander wines slumber in the cellar. For the drinker, it can offer a more supple and transparent expression of Montalcino, at a moment when freshness and immediacy matter as much as depth. In less conscientious hands, however, Rosso amounts to little more than a name on a label, and there are plenty of wineries coasting on the postcode, hoping that nobody notices – so choose carefully.

For years, Stella di Campalto's Rosso di Montalcino was my benchmark for value: a wine drawn from the same vineyards as her revered Brunello, yet released sooner and offered at a fraction of its price. Sadly, that wine no longer exists. As Stella acquired the resources to raise every bottle to Brunello maturity, she allowed the Rosso to fade into history. Today, when I'm in the mood for Rosso di Montalcino, I reach for producers such as Le Ragnaie. Its vineyards sit among the highest in the appellation, where altitude tempers Sangiovese and lends freshness to the wine's rose petal, stone and animal perfume. It's Montalcino without the armour – honest, generous and immediately rewarding.

77

Raventós i Blanc Blanc de Blancs
Individuality, Not Imitation

Region
Penedès, Spain

Grapes
Xarel·lo, Parellada, Macabeu

Price
●●○○○

ABV
12–12.5%

Food
Gambas de Palamós – some of the finest prawns in the world – grilled simply over wood smoke, Catalan-style.

Right Pepe Raventós, Penedès, Catalunya

If you make sparkling wine outside of Champagne, you must live in its shadow. The comparisons are inevitable. No serious grower wishes to be accused of imitation – of making a 'Champagne-style' wine rather than one that speaks clearly of its own soil and culture. The real challenge, then, is not to copy, but to capture individuality. Pepe Raventós's ancestors, who created Cava in 1872, mastered that balance, and today his Blanc de Blancs stands as a wine of resolutely independent character.

Some 50km west of Barcelona, Penedès is the heartland of Spanish sparkling wine, though its reputation has been tarnished by oceans of low-quality renditions, many of which have little to do with the spirit of this historic region. Cava – traditionally a blend of Xarel·lo, Parellada and Macabeu, made using the method of secondary fermentation in bottle – found international acclaim during the First World War, when Champagne had become a battlefield. In the decades since, however, its story has been co-opted by industry: vast wineries and automated lines have replaced the craft of the grower in the race to quench the world's thirst for bubbles.

In 1985, Pepe's grandfather, Josep Maria Raventós, became disillusioned with how commercial success had eroded quality at the family's historic winery, Codorníu. He sold his shares and founded Raventós i Blanc. Tragically, he died just a year after the first harvest, leaving behind both a legacy and a final act of defiance. Pepe and his father, Manuel, worked tirelessly to realise his vision and secure the winery's future. But by 2012, frustrated that Cava had come to concern itself more with process than with place, and remained largely indifferent to sustainability, Pepe withdrew from the DO altogether. In its place, he founded the Conca del Riu Anoia appellation, devoted to sparkling wines that express their origin with integrity.

And so we arrive at the inevitable comparison between Raventós i Blanc Blanc de Blancs and *Grand Marque* Champagne – though it is wiser to set this aside and taste the wine on its own terms. Farmed biodynamically, it delivers the electric snap of Penedès in an altogether higher order than the lifeless fizz produced by many of its neighbours. And if you are ever offered a glass of 'Mas del Serral' – from Pepe's tiny flagship vineyard – grab it as if it were the last drink on earth. It's a singular, finely wrought Catalan sparkling wine that proudly walks its own path.

78-79

RIDGE VINEYARDS
The Wines That Made Me Pay Attention

Three Valleys

Region
Sonoma County, California, USA

Grapes
Zinfandel, Carignan, Petite Sirah, Mataro, Alicante Bouschet

Price
●●●○○

ABV
14–14.5%

Monte Bello

Region
Santa Cruz Mountains, California, USA

Grapes
Cabernet Sauvignon, Petit Verdot, Cabernet Franc, Merlot

Price
●●●●●

ABV
13.5–14%

Food
With Ridge's reds, a simply grilled rib of beef with rosemary and olive oil is all you need.

Ridge Vineyards will always have a place at my table. One of its Zinfandels was among the first reds to show me what great wine could be. There was fruit, sure – blueberries so vivid I could picture their bloom clinging to them on the bush – but it was balanced by a savouriness unlike the wines I'd known until then. It wasn't fabricated or cosmetically polished; it didn't feel engineered, or scrubbed of its edges. Ridge wines felt alive.

Ridge became a fixture in my early days with wine. Burgundy, Bordeaux, the Rhône and the Loire Valleys followed – just a glimpse of the vast, absorbing world beyond. I'd buy two or three bottles from Roberson Wine, the independent shop a couple of doors down from Island Records, where I worked. I began attending its evening tastings. That curiosity led to Christie's and WSET diploma courses and, eventually, a fanzine about wine and the wider culture around it.

After drinking my way through Ridge's Zinfandels from Lytton Springs and Geyserville, I eventually arrived at Monte Bello – their Cabernet-dominant reference point, revered by many as California's greatest red. It's a wine I return to with undimmed pleasure year after year. Monte Bello made its name in 1976 at the Judgment of Paris tasting. There – alongside Californian wineries such as Stag's Leap Wine Cellars – it bested some of Bordeaux's leading châteaux, announcing the West Coast's arrival. Yet while Bordeaux has, at times, lost its stylistic bearings, Ridge Vineyards has remained steadfast, always aiming for restraint.

Although Ridge specialised for years in single-vineyard cuvées, around the millennium it began releasing Three Valleys – a blend of Zinfandel, Carignan, Petite Sirah, Mataro and Alicante Bouschet from Sonoma County. Full of bright fruit and that same savoury dimension that first drew me in, it's an excellent introduction to the house style.

Monte Bello is a wine for special occasions because it rises naturally to moments that matter. A first meal in a new home. A toast to success at work. Christmas Day lunch – which is when I'm writing this, with a glass in hand, as we gather to open presents. Over time, Monte Bello has found its way into some of the occasions I most want to remember.

80

Bodegas de la Riva Manzanilla Fina 'Miraflores Baja'
A Masterpiece without a Frame

Region
Sanlúcar de Barrameda, Spain

Grape
Palomino

Price
●●○○○

ABV
15%

Food
Olives, almonds, anchovies, seafood straight off the boat – this is tapas territory.

Willy Pérez and Ramiro Ibáñez didn't set out to redefine Sherry. They began by asking why it never quite aligned with the way they drank, and what had been lost when a wine once defined by terroir began to feel more like a technical process. They soon recognised a parallel between their instincts and the way Sherry was made 300 years ago, when wines were classified by site and soil rather than time in cask. Today, after reviving Bodegas de la Riva and some of its historic, long-neglected *pagos*, they are reconnecting Sherry to its long-lost, pre-industrial past – challenging assumptions about what it should be.

Bodegas de la Riva's Manzanilla Fina 'Miraflores Baja' is a bone-dry, unfortified Sherry made from fruit grown in the Miraflores Baja vineyard of Sanlúcar de Barrameda, a coastal town at the mouth of the Guadalquivir River in south-west Spain. Made from Palomino, it is aged under flor, a natural layer of yeast that protects the wine from oxidation. Sanlúcar's cool, humid, Atlantic-influenced climate allows a thicker, more persistent flor to develop than in nearby Jerez – the home of Fino – resulting in a lighter, fresher wine marked by sea breeze, green almond and chamomile (*manzanilla* in Spanish).

It does what the best aperitifs have always done – steadies the nerves, clears the head, and opens the door to whatever serious eating might follow. As Willy Pérez puts it, "Some wines are everyday or industrial; others are a work of art." 'Miraflores Baja' is firmly the latter.

CHAMPAGNE
Pol Roger
RESERVE

81

Pol Roger Brut Réserve

The Champagne That Never Needed Reinventing

Region
Champagne, France

Grapes
Pinot Noir, Pinot Meunier, Chardonnay

Price
●●○○○

ABV
12–12.5%

Food
Drink it with oysters, smoked salmon, maybe deep-fried fish. Or drink it on its own, before anyone decides what's for dinner.

Left Because one bottle was never going to cut it

So much of the talk about Champagne these days centres on its grower movement – and rightly so. But it would be a mistake to think the great houses have nothing left to say. At their best, the *Grandes Marques* still produce wines of character and complexity, shaped by generations of experience, traditions that cannot be learned overnight. It was, after all, the *négociant manipulants* – houses such as Pol Roger, Bollinger and Louis Roederer – who built Champagne's foundations and continue to sustain the region today. Their networks and accumulated *savoir-faire* created the conditions in which today's growers could find their own voice.

Pol Roger Brut Réserve has been the Champagne of choice for generations of British wine lovers, from Winston Churchill to Hugh Johnson, who called it "the perfect drink". Widely available and unfailingly delicious, it balances delicacy with richness, never tipping into sweetness. This is Champagne that feels equally at home at a wedding or Sunday lunch with friends. It has enough depth to reward attention, but it doesn't insist on it. I recently opened a Nebuchadnezzar for a milestone birthday at Noble Rot Lamb's Conduit St. Fifteen litres is a lot of Champagne. It was gone in a couple of hours.

Pol Roger is based in Épernay. Some years ago, I visited to taste one of several dozen bottles from the 1890s, excavated from a rubble-filled tunnel collapsed for more than a century, within the house's 9km of cellars. Golden in colour, with aromas of roasted hazelnuts, caramel and waxed floors, the wine's bubbles had vanished, yet its freshness and silky texture remained astonishing for a Champagne of such age. Another enduring piece of Pol Roger lore tells of the team bricking up sections of the cellar – even distressing the fresh brickwork – to hide their finest vintages from the Nazis. It's the kind of story that tells you everything about the house.

ROSÉ

Stop Drinking Whispering Angel. It's Making You Boring

Good taste isn't a lifestyle brand. It isn't a pastel-washed Instagram grid or a bottle chosen because it looks good sweating in an ice bucket on a yacht you don't own. Real pleasure comes from flavour, from specific places, from people who get their hands dirty producing a wine they've always dreamed of making.

Take Provençal rosé. No wine in the category has done better commercially than Whispering Angel. It's everywhere. Celebrity-approved. Designed to offend no one and reassure everyone. And sure – it's clean, polished, competent. But that's the problem. It's a wine engineered for certainty, not curiosity.

What it isn't is thrilling. It doesn't tell you much about where it came from, who made it, or why it matters. It's rosé as product – reliable, airbrushed and ultimately forgettable. Out there, beyond the safety rail, are rosés made by real people in real places – wines with edges, with tension, and stories behind them. They might cost less. They might taste more. They might surprise you, occasionally even challenge you. And that's the point.

Not everyone wants colour outside the lines. Some people want predictability, and that's fine. But if you're looking to escape sterile certainty – the wine equivalent of processed ready meals – the rosés that follow have actual character and zero cliché. Wines that don't need a celebrity endorsement because they've got something to say.

Left Sylvain Pataille' Marsannay Rosé 'Fleur de Pinot' (p. 199)

82

Clos Cibonne Côtes de Provence 'Cuvée Tradition' Tibouren Rosé
The Case Against Easy Rosé

Region
Provence, France

Grapes
Tibouren, Grenache

Price
●●●○○

ABV
13.5%

Food
Bouillabaisse or fish stew, grilled sardines, anchovies – this slightly oxidative wine really shines with seafood.

Domaine Tempier Bandol is my benchmark for southern French rosé, but Clos Cibonne's 'Cuvée Tradition' made me rethink the category. It's made from Tibouren, a stubborn, half-forgotten grape that's been knocking around since the dawn of civilisation – born in Mesopotamia, ferried to France by Julius Caesar, then left to sweat for centuries under the Provençal sun. When phylloxera destroyed European vineyards in the 19th century and replanting began, Tibouren – awkward, unreliable, disease-prone and notoriously difficult to farm – was mostly left behind. Too much work, not enough reward. Which is why Clos Cibonne, and the handful of growers who have refused to abandon Tibouren, matter.

Clos Cibonne organically farms Tibouren in the foothillsof the Maures mountains. The vineyards look down towards the harbour of Toulon, catching the Mediterranean sea air that has long helped shape the wines. Clos Cibonne is one of just 18 Crus Classés in Côtes de Provence, and a small proportion of Grenache is required to meet the appellation rules. It is aged in century-old *foudres*, where it rests on fine lees for a year, slowly maturing beneath a delicate veil of yeast. More copper-orange than pink, this singular wine offers wild strawberry and peach-skin notes; completely dry, it is shaped by a deep savouriness from its time under flor – a paradox of colour and character, and one of the most unique rosés being made today.

83

Faraone Cerasuolo d'Abruzzo 'Le Vigne di Faraone'

The Italian Rosé That Thinks It's a Light Red

Region
Abruzzo, Italy

Grape
Montepulciano

Price
●○○○○

ABV
14–14.5%

Food
Vitello tonnato, macaroni cheese, salami and pizza – naturally.

The difference between red and rosé wines was once obvious. Today, that line is often blurred – and frankly, when the wine is a gorgeous Cerasuolo from Abruzzo, on Italy's Adriatic coast, does it really matter? Officially a rosé, but in practice far closer to a light-bodied red, it's easy to drink lightly chilled, yet capable of real interest and evolution in the bottle. Two cult producers define the region, though both command high prices: Emidio Pepe, whose recent vintages – often served straight from the fridge – have fuelled several family holidays in Puglia; and Valentini, whose 2002 was drinking beautifully at 20 years old – still alive, still compelling, still utterly magnificent. Rosés like these belong to an older tradition, one largely forgotten amid today's industrial, marketing-led conception of the style. They prize freshness, gentle bitterness, savour, and the capacity to evolve over time.

Aside from the region's most celebrated names, a welcome option for those of us on tighter budgets is Faraone's 'Le Vigne di Faraone' Cerasuolo d'Abruzzo. It's one of those rare wines that seem to work with almost anything – cold cuts, richer dishes, fresh fruit – and is priced so sharply it feels like taking food from the Faraone children's mouths. Made from free-run juice drawn off what will later become the estate's Montepulciano d'Abruzzo, it has a lovely cherry-stone bitterness, sweet, ripe tannins, and the feel of a characterful light-bodied red – sorry, dark rosé – that repays a brief chill before serving.

84

Below Sylvain Pataille, Burgundy

Region
Burgundy, France

Grapes
Pinot Noir, Pinot Beurot

Price
●●●○○

ABV
13%

Food
From lamb cutlets and chicken kebabs to ratatouille, grilled vegetables, and niçoise-style salads.

Sylvain Pataille Marsannay Rosé 'Fleur de Pinot'
We Made It

A good wine, like a good song, can anchor a moment in time. With a single sip, you're no longer here – you're somewhere else entirely, usually a place that once mattered deeply. For me, that place is a small, temporary table outside Noble Rot, on Greek Street. It's just after midday, sunbeams ricocheting off the pavement and windows, bright enough to sting the eyes. I'm sitting alone, with time to spare before lunch, drinking Sylvain Pataille's Marsannay Rosé, 'Fleur de Pinot'. This is near the end of the third Covid-19 lockdown, in the summer of 2021 – bruised, cautious and beginning to believe we might actually make it.

The wine hits first: ripe strawberries, smoky Pinot aromatics, savoury and alive – unapologetically dark for something calling itself a rosé. And somewhere between the first sip and the last, a realisation lands: our restaurants have survived. They're still standing. Against the odds. A wine this good doesn't just taste great; it sharpens the moment. It underlines it in permanent ink. The sunlight feels brighter, the relief deeper, and the small miracle of sitting at a table in the sun suddenly enormous. 'Fleur de Pinot' isn't a rosé masquerading as something more serious, nor a Burgundy straining to impress. It's honest, assured, and quietly epic – a perfect wine for a perfect moment, made by one of the Côte d'Or's most accomplished – and, thankfully, still accessible – *vignerons*.

Based in humble Marsannay, just south of Dijon, Sylvain Pataille has helped elevate the commune the hard way: through tireless work in vineyard and domaine alike. Trained as an oenologist, he has consulted for some of Burgundy's most acclaimed estates. Yet there is nothing grandiose about his wines. From his much-loved Aligotés and Chardonnays to his Pinot Noirs, they are honest, precise and deeply satisfying – and remain among Burgundy's great bargains.

'Fleur de Pinot' is unusually versatile at the table, sitting comfortably between serious Pinot Noir and gastronomic rosé. Think refreshment with depth – not aperitif fluff.

85

Thymiopoulos Rosé de Xinomavro

What Sommeliers Drink After the Lights Go Down

Region
Macedonia, Greece

Grape
Xinomavro

Price
●○○○○

ABV
12.5%

Food
Lamb kofta, *spanakopita*, stuffed peppers, and aubergine dishes such as *imam bayildi*.

Ask Noble Rot staff what they drink when the shift's over and they want something delicious yet affordable, and one name keeps coming up: Apostolos Thymiopoulos. They might fête his Xinomavro 'Vrana Petra', which sommelier Jonah Calkin describes as "game season and summer pudding in a glass". Or rhapsodise over Naoussa 'Young Vines' – an entry-level wine that they've seen turn legions of diners onto modern Greek wine. But perhaps above all, Thymiopoulos's Rosé de Xinomavro has a special place in their hearts – "a delicious Frankenstein wine, made by the hand of a god", according to our former Soho General Manager, Emma Swift. Bursting with fresh red-berry aromatics, it pairs effortlessly with a wide range of dishes.

Xinomavro has earned cult acclaim over the past 15 years, largely through the stellar work of Apostolos Thymiopoulos and a handful of Naoussa growers. In its heartland, the grape shares affinities with Nebbiolo, albeit with a Mediterranean, olive-inflected edge. It works as convincingly as a rosé – enjoyable year-round, not just in summer. It also ages well, evident in a late-release 2009 Blanc de Rosé, made from a long-lost barrel of Xinomavro whose fermentation had stalled, before being coaxed back to life by Thymiopoulos. It proved one of the most distinctive wines we've poured by the glass, quickly becoming another staff favourite. The few cases we secured never stood a chance.

86

Fattoria San Lorenzo 'di Gino' Verdicchio

The Italian White We'd Never Give Up

Region
Marche, Italy

Grape
Verdicchio

Price
●○○○○

ABV
12.5%

Food
Anchovies, seafood, grilled vegetables, roast chicken – anything with olive oil and salt.

Every bottle poured in Noble Rot restaurants is there for a good reason. It must taste true to itself and engage both palate and mind. Our bestselling region has always been Burgundy – the wines that inspired the founding of the company. While Italian reds rank highly, Italian whites are not a category we have the same enthusiasm for. Yet Verdicchio 'di Gino' from Fattoria San Lorenzo is as Noble Rot as it gets – and has been poured since our inaugural 2014 pop-up in Ladbroke Grove. The Noble Rot Drinking Club – promising "delicious food, dubious conversation, and the finest wine list known to mankind" – featured it among the cheapest bottles. Many years later, it remains one of the greatest-value whites we pour.

Fattoria San Lorenzo sits in the Marche, on Italy's Adriatic eastern edge, in the heartland of Verdicchio. Its wines are grown in the Verdicchio dei Castelli di Jesi appellation, not far from the coast, an area capable of producing both everyday table wines and more long-lived styles. The domaine's top cuvée, 'Il San Lorenzo', is among my favourite Italian whites – textured, saline and fresh, it makes you want anchovies and a view of the sea. But for value – the kind that makes you pause, check the price again and wonder who screwed up – 'Verdicchio di Gino' is untouchable. Verdicchio is sometimes compared to Chablis or Muscadet – not because it imitates them, but because it shares their clarity and usefulness at the table. Above all, when made this well, it's a dry, citrus-fresh wine that rewards attention without demanding reverence – or a high cost of entry.

87

Below Guillaume Selosse,
Champagne

Region
Champagne, France

Grape
Chardonnay

Price
●●●●●

ABV
12.5%

Food
Jamón ibérico de bellota – the wine's umami finds its echo here.

Jacques Selosse 'Initial' Blanc de Blancs Grand Cru Brut NV
Beyond Champagne

For generations, the Champenois sold us on the idea that Champagne was more than a wine – that it was celebration itself, captured in a bottle. Then the grower revolution reminded us of something more fundamental: Champagne is first and foremost a wine, capable of the same nuance and longevity as any classic style. Yet when I drink Selosse 'Initial', made by one of the movement's true pioneers, I'm struck by how far it goes beyond even that idea. It's so singular, so deeply itself, that it seems to stand apart as a category all of its own.

'Initial' Blanc de Blancs Grand Cru Brut NV is often described as an introduction to Selosse, but that understates it. The wine contains everything that makes the domaine compelling, and with each release it seems to settle more confidently into its own voice. What draws me back, bottle after bottle, is the way it seems to reconcile opposites. There's the saline, savoury depth you find in biologically aged wines such as Vin Jaune and Manzanilla, but carried on bubbles that are unmistakably Côte des Blancs: fine, chalky and precise. Chardonnay from Avize, Cramant and Oger gives the wine its spine, but it's the *élevage* that helps it truly find its voice.

Anselme Selosse, who built his father's domaine reputation, left Champagne for Beaune in his twenties, where he learned what his home region had forgotten: that great wines are grown from the ground up, not imposed from the label down. In the early 1970s, visits to López de Heredia in Rioja and the Sherry *bodegas* of Jerez taught him how extra time in barrel could give a wine a depth no dosage could replace. He began fermenting all his wines with indigenous yeasts in oak, letting them breathe and gain texture, and – drawing on what he had seen in Spain – embraced gentle oxidative ageing, sometimes with a protective veil of yeast cells forming on their surface.

Closer in spirit to a Burgundian grower than to a Champagne *Grande Marque*, by the late 1970s he was practising what he calls *agriculture de respect*: working the soil, avoiding herbicides, encouraging biodiversity and treating the vineyard as a living organism – ideas that were radical at the time. Today, Anselme's son Guillaume has taken the reins. Few would envy the task of following such an influential father, but the early signs suggest this may be one of those rare cases in which the son carries the family legacy even higher. 'Initial' was once the most conventional of the Selosse cuvées, but under his guidance it has become the quintessential expression of the house.

88

Suertes del Marqués 'Trenzado'
White Heat from a Black Island

Region
Tenerife, Spain

Grapes
Listán Blanco, other varieties

Price
●●○○○

ABV
12.5%

Food
Octopus straight off the grill with olive oil, lemon and smoked paprika – the char and sweetness of the flesh answering the wine's smoky, mineral edge.

On Tenerife's north coast, vineyards still run down to the sea. Standing above the Atlantic, it's easy to imagine British galleons anchoring here in the 17th century, when this volcanic island was a vital port of call for ships bound for the New World – and a prodigious source of wine in its own right. Fresh water rarely survived long sea voyages, so sailors lived by the cask rather than the jug. Having acquired a taste for Tenerife's wines, British and Irish merchants began importing them in vast quantities – as much as 15 million litres a year at the height of the island's success.

Tenerife's wine trade fell away after the 1830s under mounting competition, its vineyards largely forgotten. Nearly 200 years later, Suertes del Marqués, along with a handful of others, is producing beautiful, smoky-mineral whites from ancient Listán Blanco vines (known as Palomino in Jerez), rooted in black volcanic slopes, alongside a range of reds. These are not new wines so much as old ones recalled – honest, grounded, and entirely in tune with the modern appetite for freshness and restraint.

'Trenzado', the gateway to Suertes del Marqués' whites, has an alluring smokiness that recalls the savoury crunch of those childhood crisps, Frazzles – an aroma winemaker Jonatan García Lima attributes to the island's volcanic soils. Year after year it consistently shines: a fine wine delivering complexity and depth far above its pay grade, tasting more like it's born of stone than pressed from fruit (not unlike Chenin Blanc). The name 'Trenzado' refers to *cordón trenzado*, a rare system of vine training in which canes are woven back into twisted old trunks and raised on poles, creating long, braided forms that trace the contours of the Valle de la Orotava.

A lost classic, brought back to life – and a measure of how far Spanish fine white wine has come.

Left Tending cordón trenzado–trained vines, Valle de la Orotava, Tenerife

Right Vines trained in cordón trenzado, Valle de la Orotava, Tenerife

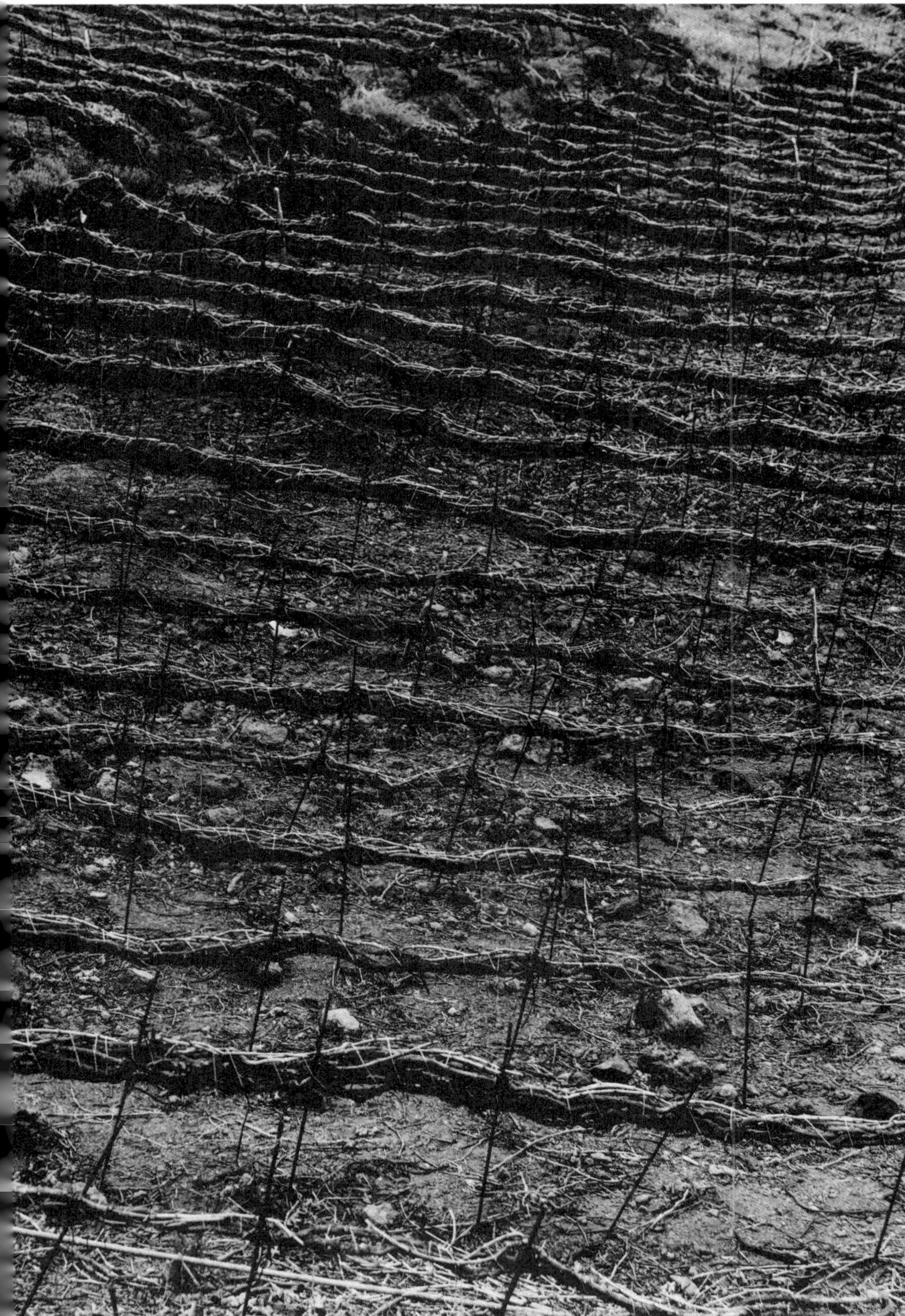

89

Below Priorat, Catalunya

Region
Priorat, Spain

Grapes
Cariñena, Garnacha

Price
●●○○○

ABV
13.5%

Food
Drink this with lamb chops grilled over charcoal – 'Històric' doesn't want clever food, just something honest to lean against.

Terroir al Límit Soc. Lda. 'Històric' Tinto

When Catalunya Learned to Levitate

No one knows whether psilocybin mushrooms inspired the shepherd's vision of angels ascending a ladder to heaven – the 12th-century founding myth of Scala Dei, the monastery where winemaking in Priorat began. Much later, when a young German named Dominik Huber showed up in this remote, vertiginous and thoroughly unfashionable corner of Catalunya, 140km west of Barcelona, more than a few locals might have wondered what kind of vision he was following.

He called his project Terroir al Límit, a nod to the place's austerity – no phone signal, no internet, not even a café for a morning fry-up – and set about crafting wines of rare delicacy in a region long associated with blockbuster power. At first, many locals laughed at Huber's early harvesting in pursuit of freshness, his rigorous sorting of fruit, and his obsessive attention to detail. His wines were even rejected by the Priorat DOCa board – Spain's highest appellation, shared only with Rioja – for being atypical. Yet their brilliance was hard to deny.

Farming native grapes biodynamically, he embraced whole-cluster fermentations to produce spicy, ethereal perfumes and the gentlest of extractions, allowing flavour to infuse rather than be forced. The resulting wines stand in striking contrast to the swaggering, oak-laden alcohol bombs of international grapes that had won Priorat fame in the 1990s.

'Històric' Tinto, is a gorgeous introduction to his style made from Garnacha and Cariñena grown around Priorat's nine villages. It defies expectations of such a hot, arid landscape: light, bright and fresh, full of herbs, flowers and the region's slaty minerality.

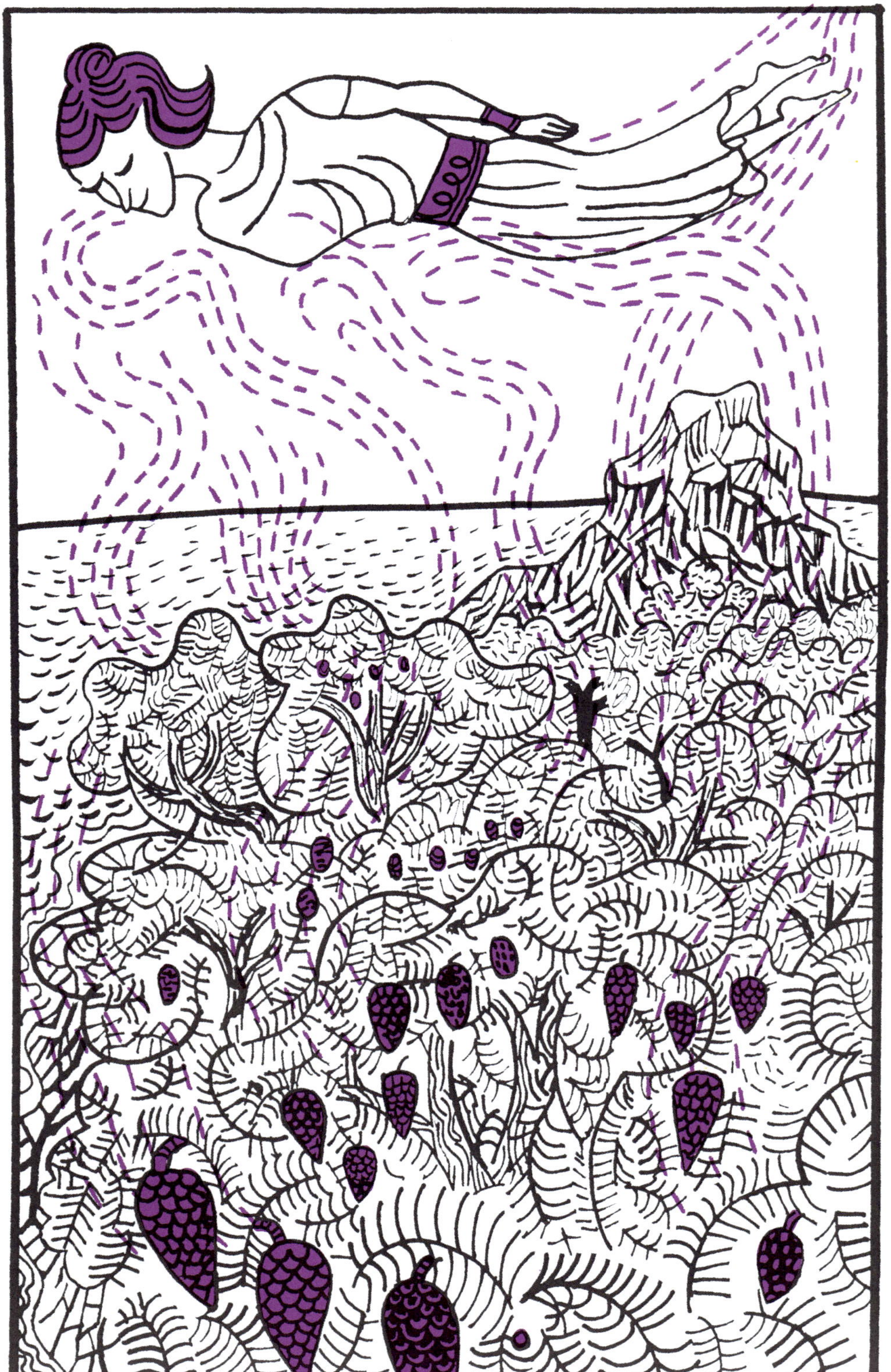

90

Tetramythos Retsina Amphore Natur
A Very Ancient Mistake

Region
Peloponnese, Greece

Grape
Roditis

Price
●○○○○

ABV
12%

Food
Grilled sardines with lemon and olive oil work wonders, with Retsina's fresh, piny edge lifting the fish and making everything taste brighter and more appetising.

Like many traditions, Retsina began as a mistake. Greece's love-it-or-loathe-it contribution to drinking history, this resin-scented wine has survived from antiquity – sometimes, it seems, in spite of itself. The ancients sealed amphorae with pine resin, which scented the wine; over time, people grew accustomed to the flavour, and came to expect it. Before long, accident became intention – and once pine was accepted, so too were honey, spices, even the odd cheese rind. Ancient wine was not the pristine ideal we imagine, but a more inventive playground of additions — one of which still survives as Retsina.

Of course, not all Retsina is a story of rebirth. Much of it tastes like pine air freshener – an ordeal holidaymakers endure from plastic jugs at seaside tavernas. But the best versions can be aromatic and implausibly good with a table crowded with sharing dishes. Panagiotis Papagiannopoulos of Tetramythos Winery, in the northern Peloponnese, makes the only single-vineyard Retsina: Roditis grapes from a single plot, matched with resin from the surrounding pines. The north-facing vineyard – a rarity in Greece – sits high on Mount Aroania, overlooking the Gulf of Corinth, while the entire operation is grounded in organic farming, spontaneous fermentations, and a side project devoted to reviving forgotten grapes.

The resin traditionally comes from pine trees on the island of Evia. It's still harvested much as it always was: a cut in the bark, a metal spout, a container catching the sticky drips. It's artisanal in the most literal sense – little more than careful tree-tapping – and for centuries winemakers have bought it directly from these resin farmers. Retsina's base is usually Savatiano. Long sneered at as a rustic also-ran, it can, when handled with care, deliver something delicious. Roditis often plays a supporting role. More recently, a new generation has arrived: boutique producers experimenting with Assyrtiko, using resin tea bags, and pricing the results to match their ambition.

Retsina's renaissance mirrors Greek wine's own reinvention over the past decade or two. It remains an acquired taste, certainly – but then so are anchovies and negronis, among life's true glories. The ancients relished their flavoured wines, and Retsina endures as one of the few surviving threads: not quite a relic, but an eccentric tradition made modern, and a reminder that the past still has something to say – if we're willing to taste it.

91

Domaine Camille Thiriet Bourgogne 'En la Place'
No Inheritance Required

Region
Burgundy, France

Grape
Pinot Noir

Price
●●●●○

ABV
12.5%

Food
I'd be happy with *coq au vin*, or even a lentil and walnut salad – dishes that meet the wine on its own ground, without trying to upstage it.

Right Camille Thiriet, Burgundy

Like the neglected corners of cities that find new life, Burgundy has known its own cycles of decline and renewal. When Camille Thiriet made her first vintage from grapes purchased in Côte de Nuits-Villages in 2016, the appellation was little known. More than a decade later, she and her Canadian husband, Matt Chittick, farm 6ha, producing characterful wines that have drawn fresh attention to a long-overlooked corner of the Côte d'Or.

Thiriet belongs to a growing group of outsiders who have come to Burgundy to learn its craft. When she enrolled at the wine school in Beaune, surrounded by the children of established *vignerons*, she admits she did not yet grasp how difficult it would be to create a domaine, rather than inherit one. After years spent sourcing fruit and piecing together parcels of vines, she and Chittick made a decisive move in 2022, acquiring Domaine Gilles Jourdan in Corgoloin and transforming the scale of their estate.

I've enjoyed watching Thiriet's wines gain in stature and finesse over recent vintages, shaped in part by guidance from figures such as Bernard Noblet, former winemaker at Domaine de la Romanée-Conti, and Jérémy Seysses of Domaine Dujac. With Burgundy prices continuing to rise, Thiriet's Bourgogne 'En la Place', from old vines just beyond the Côte de Nuits-Villages boundary, is a canny place to begin. One of the signatures of her wines is whole-bunch fermentation – stems and all – a choice that lends them a natural spice and floral lift. It's not unlike what you find a few miles up the road at Domaine de la Romanée-Conti, where the same practice helps give its Grands Crus that ineffable perfume and vitality.

THIRIET

92

Château des Tours Côtes du Rhône Rouge
A More Practical Alternative to the Perfect Wine

Region
Southern Rhône Valley, France

Grapes
Grenache, Syrah, Cinsault

Price
●●●●●

ABV
14.5%

Food
This is a wine that asks for simplicity at the table. A roast guinea fowl, a rack of lamb or a ragù of wild mushrooms will do just fine.

I ask myself what I'd bring if I were marooned for Radio 4's *Desert Island Discs*. After the obligatory Bible and the complete works of Shakespeare, the answer comes easily: a cellar full of Château Rayas. It's a wine that refuses to behave like any other, and that's why it lodges deeply in the memory. I've spent years chasing down bottles when luck, generosity or benevolent pricing aligned, and each time the spell has held. Rayas doesn't fade with familiarity; it deepens. You simply understand it a little better – until the bottle is empty, and you start wondering when you'll encounter it again.

Mythical wines have a way of feeding on scarcity. You hear about them endlessly, but almost no one seems to drink them. Rayas is different: it's costly, but it's there for those who are patient, and it does deliver.

What makes Rayas compelling is not a dramatic gesture, but a series of refusals. It comes from Châteauneuf-du-Pape, an appellation that has drifted, over the years, towards wines built more on ripeness and alcohol than on pleasure at the table – yet Rayas remains one of the most coveted bottles in the world. And while Châteauneuf traditionally allows for a sprawling blend of grapes, Rayas is Grenache, and only Grenache. A grape long dismissed as rustic, here reveals a depth, grace and staying power that few people thought it capable of. It sits there in the glass, insisting that everything you thought you knew might be wrong.

Rayas stands on sand, an anomaly in Châteauneuf-du-Pape, where most vineyards are strewn with *galets roulés* – pudding stones that soak up the sun and contribute to the overripe excess of its neighbours. One of Rayas's former owners, Louis Reynaud, cleared them away, helping the wines to stay lighter on their feet. The cellar is no less idiosyncratic: barrels stacked wherever they fit, no cosmetic gestures, no sense that anyone ever tried to impress a visitor. Over the years, rumours have circulated that spices or citrus peel find their way into the barrels. I've never seen evidence of this, but taste the wine and you understand why people start telling themselves that story. 1978 Rayas is one of the greatest reds I've drunk – a high-cheekboned, statuesque yet generous wine, still pulsing with life after all these years.

Emmanuel Reynaud, Louis's nephew, used to say that Rayas needed time to find its footing. His advice was to pour out a small glass, replace the cork, and leave it somewhere cool for three days before drinking. I've followed that advice, and it has never failed – most recently with a bottle of 2006 Rayas, opened over Easter. We drank a glass on Good Friday, another on Saturday, and one more on Sunday – an act of restraint that felt almost theological. Each day the wine grew more expressive, unfurling into that unmistakable Rayas register: strawberries and kirsch, a dusting of white pepper, and a faint scent of rose petals.

Let's get this out of the way: Rayas is not cheap. Not remotely. If it were a band, it'd be playing CBGB but charging Madison Square Garden prices. Current releases start in the hundreds, and if you start digging into the 1980s or '70s, the numbers get stupid fast. That's the price of obsession, scarcity and people who know exactly what they're doing. The good news – because there's always good news in today's wine culture if you're paying attention – is that the Reynaud family makes another wine nearby that lets you explore a little of that Rayas magic at a more civilised price. Château des Tours Rouge is a bright, rich red that shares more DNA with Rayas than seems reasonable for the price, and while it doesn't possess the same dimensions as its illustrious sibling, some vintages get tantalisingly close.

CRIADERA
AMONTILLAD
1/22

93

Bodegas Tradición Cream VOS 20 Years

The Redemption of Cream Sherry

Region
Jerez de la Frontera, Spain

Grapes
Palomino Fino, Pedro Ximénez

Price
●●●●○

ABV
18.5%

Food
Bodegas Tradición Cream VOS is an ideal pairing for dark chocolate and raisin-and-nut desserts, from tiffin to ice cream.

When our sommelier Ana Rey floated the idea of adding a cream Sherry to the wine list, the team reacted as if she'd proposed microwaved ramen as the restaurant's new signature dish. The office fell silent, a few awkward smiles betraying the fact that cream Sherry had already been mentally consigned to the dusty shelf where forgotten styles go to die.

Ana, however, had tasted something different. Rather than argue, she simply poured the wine for the team, without revealing what was in their glass. Freed from preconceptions, their palates responded with unexpected enthusiasm, recognising how the wine's sweetness and *rancio* character fell into an effortless harmony. Ana insists she never intended to list *a* cream Sherry; she intended to list *this* cream Sherry, from Bodegas Tradición, because it transcends the category. Taste it, and the distinction is immediately obvious.

Though re-established only in 1998, Bodegas Tradición draws on Jerez's rich winemaking heritage, dedicating itself to the preservation of rare, exceptionally mature Sherries. Set in the historic heart of the town, its atmospheric buildings, rows of venerable *botas*, and even its own art collection give the place more the air of a museum than a working winery. Rather than producing wine from scratch, the *bodega* has focused on sourcing, acquiring and ageing exceptional old barrels, and curating and bottling them as some of Jerez's most coveted releases. A tour of the cellars offers more than a tasting alone: it's an immersion in Sherry tradition, time-worn casks and artisanal craftsmanship.

Most cream Sherries are blended from young, forgettable wines, but Bodegas Tradición's Cream VOS is a different proposition, averaging more than 20 years of age. It begins with an old Oloroso – mahogany-dark, all walnuts, dried fruit and slow, oxygen-fed patience – before a measure of Pedro Ximénez is blended in, that dark, sun-soaked raisin elixir. Not a sticky shortcut, but a true old-fashioned cream: deep, decadent, and astonishing with chocolate desserts. It leaves you wondering why the style ever fell out of favour.

Left Bodegas Tradición, Jerez de la Frontera

94

Below Nicola Oberto, Trediberri, Piedmont

Next spread Piedmont

Region
Piedmont, Italy

Grape
Nebbiolo

Price
●●●○○

ABV
14.5%

Food
Tajarin with shaved white truffle, or mushroom risotto – dishes that echo Nebbiolo's savoury depth without overwhelming its perfume.

Trediberri Barolo 'Berri'
A Barolo for Now

Nicola Oberto doesn't just talk; he *erupts*. He rises, crouches, and sweeps his arms through the air like he's conducting an unseen orchestra. His voice accelerates as if chasing a scooter through Milan, then tumbles over itself, trying to catch up with whatever thought he's trying to pin down. It's wonderfully Italian – and you understand him perfectly long before the words land. At Trediberri, he makes Barolos you want to drink rather than admire, offering remarkable value.

Barolo is a famous appellation tucked into the misty hills of north-west Italy that has weathered a revolution – one that reshaped not just how its red wines are made, but how the people there understand their land and their craft. Decades ago, many of these Nebbiolos had a rusticity – stern, unyielding wines with piercing acidity and feisty tannins that demanded patience before revealing their beauty.

Then came the 1990s, and with them modernisation: French oak *barriques* rolled in, the old *botti* were pushed aside, and winery technology began rounding off Nebbiolo's edges. For years, producers argued about what the soul of these wines was supposed to be. Tasting here today, though, those extremes seem largely behind us. A generation of growers such as Trediberri is crafting balanced Barolos with sensual perfumes and firm but finely shaped tannins that feel true to the place.

Trediberri's cellar sits in La Morra, a commune known for Barolos that favour finesse over power. From its doorstep, it looks out over 'Rocche dell'Annunziata', an amphitheatre of vines regarded as one of La Morra's crown jewels. This is where the late Lorenzo Accomasso made legendary bottles in his idiosyncratic, stubborn way, and where Trediberri now adds its own clear, honest touch. But whereas 'Rocche dell'Annunziata's reputation rests on structured wines with layers of flavour that take years to unfold, Trediberri's nearby Berri vineyard delivers immediate pleasure.

Berri is a high-altitude site thriving in a warming climate. It may not yield the complexity of 'Rocche dell'Annunziata' but it produces bright, classically shaped wines without the old, hard-edged austerity. Nicola's focus is on purity of fruit – the difference between a tomato ripened in Sicily and one raised under plastic in Scotland – yielding a Barolo that is silky, generous, yet always serious.

95

Union of Winemaking Cooperatives of Samos Nectar
Cut the Gods Some Slack

Region
Samos, Greece

Grape
Muscat

Price
●●○○○

ABV
14%

Food
Drink this with salty cheeses – from Roquefort to Parmigiano Reggiano – where the wine's honeyed richness meets resistance and comes alive. It's also beautiful with desserts made from nuts or dried fruit, but just as often I prefer it on its own.

We live in a world hooked on sugar, yet wary of sweetness in wine. It's everywhere – in cereals, fizzy drinks, desserts cooked up in laboratories – but pour someone a traditional sweet wine and they look at you as if you've handed them cough syrup. Centuries ago, life was hard, often brutal, and flavour, especially of the sugary kind, was a rare luxury. Imagine, then, someone pouring you a glass of luscious Samos Nectar, its sweetness born of sun and soil rather than a factory line. You take a sip and, for a moment, it feels like a miracle, as if the gods have finally cut you a little slack.

The island of Samos produces Greece's most renowned sweet wine. Given the labour involved, it remains one of the wine world's best values. Its story is, fittingly, the stuff of legend. Once famed for red wines, Samos was abandoned to pirates in the 15th century and lay desolate for generations, until its Ottoman rulers encouraged resettlement. The returning islanders planted Muscat – believed to be the oldest grape still cultivated by humankind – and in doing so helped restore both livelihood and identity. Today, vines cling to the island's steep, terraced granite slopes, giving the wines their freshness and intensity.

Samos Muscat spans a range of sweetness levels, from the light Grand Cru to the oak-aged Anthemis, culminating in the island's crown jewel, Nectar. Made from sun-dried grapes and aged for six years in old oak barrels, the unfortified Nectar is amber-hued, and luxurious on the palate. In its youth, it tastes of honey, raisins, toasted nuts and spice – a wine to drink in place of dessert, especially with a well-chosen cheeseboard. With time, its magic only deepens. A late-release 1963 from the Union of Winemaking Cooperatives of Samos was one of those wines that recalibrates your expectations. Gloriously fresh despite its age, it was also rich and many-layered, unfolding slowly and lingering on the senses long after the glass was empty.

96

Below Gérard Courrèges,
Domaine de Vaccelli, Corsica

Region
Ajaccio, Corsica

Grapes
Carcaghjolu Bianco, Ghjenuvese, Cudiverta, Riminese

Price
●●●●○

ABV
13.5%

Food
Grilled fish – sea bream or red mullet – makes the perfect foil.

Domaine de Vaccelli 'Quartz' Blanc

Before You Know Its Name

When we opened our first restaurant, we adopted a ritual at the end of dinner service. The sommeliers took turns disappearing into the cellar and re-emerging with a mystery bottle and a mischievous glint, pouring it for the rest of the team without a word of introduction. For debutants wondering what price point to aim for, my business partner Mark offered a guideline: "Don't be a pussy. Don't be a dick."

With older wines, context and story are half the pleasure. With young ones, blind tasting becomes something else entirely: an invitation to judge a wine's character and its ability to speak for itself before you know its name.

More than ten years on, I join those after-service tastings less often than I'd like, but the last time I did, a Corsican white blend rose above the rest with such clarity that I can still see its silhouette. Domaine de Vaccelli's 'Quartz' – a wine as stony as its name suggests, shaped by granite and sun – seemed to command the room's attention in a single moment. If you're looking for something with the refinement of a top Chablis, yet unmistakably different, this might be the wine for you.

Corsica's artisanal white-wine production is booming to meet rising demand, with Vermentinu its star. But the Mountain in the Sea has plenty more to offer besides. Four of its lesser-known native varieties – Carcaghjolu Bianco, Ghjenuvese, Cudiverta and Riminese (your guess is as good as mine) – are harnessed to magnificent effect in 'Quartz' Blanc.

Tucked into the Ajaccio AOC, Domaine de Vaccelli is the work of Gérard Courrèges, a lover of Cuban cigars with a Burgundian sensibility, committed to letting each of his hillside parcels speak for itself. The result is a set of single-vineyard wines that seem hewn from Corsica's granite and maquis, their stark, no-nonsense labels the sort you recognise from across a crowded cellar.

97

Verget Mâcon-Pierreclos 'Lieu Secret'
No Grand Cru, No Problem

Region
Burgundy, France

Grapes
Chardonnay

Price
●●○○○

ABV
13%

Food
The best chicken you can find, gently cooked with mushrooms and cream, served with rice pilaf.

Right Jean-Marie Guffens, Noble Rot, Lamb's Conduit Street

Sitting here with a glass of Verget Mâcon-Pierreclos 'Lieu Secret', I'm carried back to a Hampstead carpet shop I wandered into yesterday. The owner, who spoke of furnishings with the gravity of a monk discussing manuscripts, explained that my chosen carpet was offered in the same weave in different depths, from a modest single pile to something into which you could lose your toes. It reminded me that Burgundy operates on a similar principle: the deeper you go, the more you pay, the more you're meant to feel. But every so often, someone ignores the hierarchy entirely – and makes something that unsettles the scale.

Jean-Marie Guffens is one of those people, and Mâcon-Pierreclos 'Lieu Secret' one such wine. While it doesn't quite have the depth or lace-like precision of his top Mâconnais Chardonnays – Crus capable of outshining many Montrachets – its quality and price are remarkable, not least given that its fruit comes from the only grower other than Guffens in the mighty Chavigne vineyard. Verget is Guffens's *négociant* business (which purchases grapes rather than farming them, unlike Domaine Guffens-Heynen), and 'Lieu Secret' is a lightly disguised reference to this source of fruit. Like all Verget wines, it's white Burgundy for people who don't feel like paying white Burgundy prices.

Guffens's career has been defined by extremes: soaring acclaim, fierce resistance, and ordeals that would have broken most people. From the beginning, his path was unconventional. When he and his wife, Maine Heynen, came down from Belgium to the Mâconnais in 1976, they brought plenty of optimism, little formal training, and a natural mistrust of orthodoxies. Wine school taught him methods he would later dismiss; his own pragmatic, chemical-free approach set him on a different course.

WINE BAR

His purchase of 'Chavigne' in the town of Pierreclos marked the start of the ascent. The vineyard was unwanted – too steep and without pedigree – but Guffens saw potential where others didn't. By 1982 his wines were attracting attention, and suddenly the outsider from Belgium was being mentioned alongside producers from far grander terroirs. The late 1980s and early '90s brought a run of extraordinary vintages, and the creation of Verget accelerated his rise. Access to top fruit, audacious winemaking and critical praise propelled him forward, even as debts mounted and the pressure intensified.

The near collapse, when it came, was brutal. A bewildering and prolonged fraud-squad investigation – raids, false accusations of illegal blending, and administrative chaos – pushed Guffens to the edge. Years of work were threatened by baseless claims, and the emotional toll was immense. When the case finally fell apart in 2011, he emerged exhausted but undefeated. Today, his wines are better than ever: tense, textural, mineral whites that rank among the world's finest. With an instinctive touch and a refusal to cut corners, he remains the sort of winemaker who won't dilute a principle any more than he would a cuvée – uncompromising in wine, as in life.

Left Mâconnais vineyards, with Guffens's top plot 'Clos des Petits-Croux' in the centre background

98

Domaine Jean-Marc Vincent Santenay Blanc 'Les Vignes Denses'

Montrachet Talent, Santenay Prices

Region
Burgundy, France

Grape
Chardonnay

Price
●●●○○

ABV
13%

Food
A simple crab salad with lemon and herbs is ideal here, the wine's brightness and mineral edge lifting the crab's natural sweetness without overwhelming its delicacy.

Burgundy, when it's honest, is about place. Not as an abstraction, but as a living fact – the soil underfoot, exposure to the sun, and the weather of a particular year. Certain vineyards have earned fame because they deliver greatness with remarkable consistency. But reputation alone has never made a wine worth drinking. A grand site is a gift, not a guarantee. Anyone can bottle Montrachet and ask a small fortune. The real measure of a grower is what they do with humbler ground. That's where you find the *vignerons* listening closely, working thoughtfully, and refusing shortcuts. Growers like Jean-Marc Vincent prove that distinction in Burgundy isn't reserved for the exalted Crus. They make wines of character and energy, priced as if pleasure, not prestige, were still the point.

Vincent, a farming-obsessed grower in his fifties, is based in the pretty but often overlooked commune of Santenay, in the Côte de Beaune. Once a prosperous spa town whose vineyards ranked among the region's best, Santenay slipped into relative obscurity in the wake of phylloxera at the end of the 19th century. Today, Vincent is helping to restore its standing through rigorous viticulture – lowering yields and planting at high density to encourage plant competition and produce more concentrated fruit.

Santenay Blanc 'Les Vignes Denses'– from one such parcel, planted at 14,000 vines per hectare – is a strikingly pure, finely drawn white: racy, floral and persistent.

When a grower can coax this level of detail from an unassuming site, it's hard not to wonder what they might be capable of elsewhere. Wines like this have a way of reordering hierarchies.

99-100

YELLOW WINE
Wine with No Interest in Pleasing You

François Rousset-Martin Château-Chalon

Region
Jura, France

Grape
Savagnin

Price
●●●●●

ABV
15%

Food
Yellow wine is heaven with Comté and Mont d'Or, as it is with the godlike Jura classic, chicken with morels and Vin Jaune sauce, a mainstay of our Soho restaurant's menu.

Left Vin jaune and Comté cheese

Do you remember your first anchovy? The shock of salt and brine, far removed from the easy comforts of butter or bread. Or the first time you tasted an olive, or a dab of lime pickle? Flavours that didn't seek your approval, that demanded you meet them on their own terms. Vin Jaune is the wine-world equivalent – sui generis, anathema to some, irresistible to others. It's an acquired pleasure: strange at first, but deepening each time you return.

Four Jura appellations – Arbois, Côtes du Jura, L'Étoile and Château-Chalon – are allowed to make Vin Jaune ('Yellow Wine'), but only Château-Chalon is devoted to it entirely. From high on its limestone promontory, the village looks out across the foothills of the French Alps like a custodian of tradition. Vin Jaune is often spoken of in terms of power, and the austerity born from Savagnin's long oxidation. Yet François Rousset-Martin's Château-Chalons are defined by finesse – layers of unexpected flavour that reveal themselves with patience and air. From waxed floors and toast to peat, iodine, celery, fruitcake, fenugreek, even mango, the flavours unfurl endlessly.

Yellow wine is made by arcane means. Savagnin – powerful, high in acid, often picked late, when the days are short and the air smells of smoke and earth – is fermented dry, then left to rest in old 228-litre Burgundy barrels for at least six years and three months – often longer.

In most cellars a winemaker would guard against oxygen, topping up each barrel as the wine evaporates. But here, the cask is left unfilled, a small pocket of air permitted to do its work. And then, as if by design, a thin *voile* –

Left François Rousset-Martin, Jura

a veil of yeast, like the flor that forms on Sherry – spreads across the surface, protecting the wine from oxidation while transforming it into something deeper, more mysterious. This is called 'biological ageing'.

François Rousset-Martin raises his Château-Chalon in a cellar that feels more like a crypt than a winery. The air is thick with the scent of yeast and stone; barrels and bottles wear a soft bloom of mould, as though time itself has taken up residence. Rousset-Martin speaks of wine as emotion, the invisible microbial life of his cellar as vital as soil or sun to its finished character. Where many others scrub their caves into sterility, he believes something is lost – that wine raised in antiseptic conditions is wine without feeling.

Château-Chalon is served at cellar temperature, either as an aperitif – with a few walnuts, perhaps – or at the end of a meal, alongside the local Comté or Mont d'Or, which echo its umami character. This is not a wine for everyone. It is rare, and asks a great deal of the drinker. But give it time – surrender to its otherness – and it answers. Each time I drink it, I'm reminded that the wines I love most never stop surprising me.

Domaine Macle Côtes du Jura

Region
Jura, France

Grapes
Chardonnay, Savagnin

Price
●●●○○

ABV
13–14%

Food
Sous voile ('under the veil') wines are extraordinarily versatile. This pairs beautifully with everything from tandoori to ramen.

Located in cool, cavernous cellars beneath Château-Chalon, Domaine Macle is one of the Jura's historic domaines, making wine with the calm assurance of those who know what they're entrusted with. Its Château-Chalon – a long-aged Vin Jaune capable of living for decades – remains the estate's defining wine, but it also produces a Côtes du Jura that offers a gentler way in. A blend of Chardonnay and Savagnin that spends less time under flor than its loftier sibling, it carries the same oxidative notes in a softer, more yielding register. It's a natural starting point for those curious about Jura wines, not yet ready for the full intensity of Château-Chalon.

HOW TO SERVE WINE

Wine Can Survive Frost, Mildew, War and Bureaucracy. What It Cannot Survive Is Bad Service

Given the obscene amount of labour, patience, luck, heartbreak and near-religious devotion that goes into making a beautiful bottle of wine, it is remarkable how easily it can all be undone at the final moment. Restaurants will proudly pour a revered Cru into a stubby bistro glass – the vinous equivalent of viewing a Rothko under strip lighting – while some sommeliers, sleeves rolled up with missionary zeal, decant ancient bottles without asking, even when they have only minutes of glory left before collapsing into an oxidised whisper. Congratulations: you have missed the point entirely.

Then there are the three-star mausoleums that won't let you anywhere near the bottle you've ordered, treating wine like a controlled substance, rationing it out in thimblefuls or topping up your glass the moment you take a sip. Worse still are restaurants that haven't trained their staff, administering the 'trucker pour' to just below the rim, with all the finesse of a motorway coffee refill. These places – places that confuse control with hospitality – deserve a special corner of hell. Preferably one with warm Prosecco and glasses that smell of rinse aid.

Serving wine is not a footnote; it is a critical cog in the machinery of pleasure – or misery – depending on who is in charge.

Temperature Is Not a Suggestion

One of the worst crimes against wine is committed at the thermostat. Reds arrive warm, bloated and alcoholic, sweating in the glass like they've just come off a long-haul flight. The ritual of serving them at 'room temperature' was coined in draughty 19th-century country houses, not centrally heated apartments. Give them a short stint in the fridge – 15 minutes is enough – to rein in the alcohol, sharpen the edges and help the fruit taste fresher. Light-bodied reds and rosés show best around 12°C (54°F), with fuller styles somewhere between that and a maximum of 18°C (64°F).

Whites, meanwhile, are often served so cold they might as well be anaesthetised. This is tolerable for cheap industrial wines, whose limited charms you're unlikely to mask anyway, but a disaster for anything made with care. The ideal serving temperature for whites lies between 7°C (45°F) and 14°C (57°F), Champagne at the cooler end, serious whites at the other. Served too cold, a beautiful Burgundy will taste muted, its acidity exaggerated. Take it out of the fridge 20 minutes before serving and let it wake up.

If you need to chill a bottle quickly, don't just bury it in ice. Use ice and water. Ice chills by contact; water conducts the cold evenly, avoiding a frozen shoulder and a lukewarm core.

Don't Shake the Bottle

It may sound like common sense – believe me, it isn't – but be careful not to shake a bottle that contains sediment on the way to the table. If the wine is mature, let it stand upright for a few hours, or even days, before opening so the sediment can settle.

The waiter's friend remains the most useful everyday tool for opening a bottle: a small blade to pare away the capsule, a screw, and a simple lever that does the job without fuss. When dealing with older wines whose corks have grown fragile, the Durand is unequalled. It is not a luxury so much as an act of mercy, and anyone serious about wine will want one at hand.

Some *vignerons* seal their bottles with wax, less for show than for protection. Ignore the temptation to chip at it. Instead, drive the screw through the wax and into the cork, pull steadily, and let the seal break as it comes away.

Always check a wine's condition before serving, because not every bottle arrives as its maker intended. Trust your nose: damp cardboard, vinegar, bruised apples, barnyard, or cooked fruit aromas signal cork taint, oxidation, heat damage, or microbial spoilage – and it's better to move on than to make excuses for a bottle that's lost its way.

In Its Own Time

When you open a bottle matters. Wine isn't a switch you flip – it's more like a conversation, and if you rush it, you'll often miss the good part. Open a young wine and pour it straight away and it can feel tight, stingy, half-asleep. Walk away, come back a few hours later, and suddenly it's loosened its tie: fruit and floral aromas blooming, tannins softening, the whole thing finally acting like it trusts you.

Even young reds that are meant to be 'ready to drink' can benefit from air – sometimes a lot of it. Decanting can help, but there are no rules here, and living wine doesn't care about your timetable. Some bottles wake up quickly, show well for an hour, then shut down again just to mess with you. So open the bottle early. Taste it. If it needs help, decant it. If it's cruising, stick the cork halfway back in and return later.

I've learned the hard way that many quality white wines under a decade old love oxygen. Open one the night before a dinner, pour yourself half a glass – call it quality control – and put the bottle in the fridge. Time and again it comes back the next day more expressive, with better texture and gears you didn't know were there. Try this with plenty of reds, though, and the results are less reliable. Often they return flatter, a little less alive.

Older whites are trickier. The line between just enough and too much air is thin, and if a wine is already on its last legs, oxygen can finish it off fast. With very old bottles, you have to be present when they open. Sometimes you get a few minutes of brilliance and that's it. Miss it, and it's gone. Don't decant them by default – and the same goes for very old reds.

Many fine wines are judged too quickly, before they've had the air they need to reveal themselves. Restaurants, in particular, are difficult places for young bottles: the pace is fast, expectations are immediate, and patience is in short supply. There is no real way to hurry a living wine along, whatever the claims made for aerators and other contraptions. Wine opens in its own time.

That said, guests will sometimes ring or email ahead to ask that a bottle be opened in advance, and it can make all the difference, for better or worse. Many growers – particularly in Barolo and Brunello di Montalcino – will tell you their wines should never be decanted, that following their evolution in the glass is part of the pleasure. And yet Emmanuel Reynaud recommended opening his legendary Château Rayas wines three days before drinking, allowing them to soar. There are no hard-and-fast rules. Living wines must be judged on their own terms.

The Right Glass

Most of what you're tasting is smell, so don't drown the glass. Pour it no more than halfway – often less – so the wine has room to open up and you can get your nose in there. The glass matters more than most people realise: the wrong one lets a wine's aromas drift away, while the right one gathers and focuses them.

A proper wine glass should be plain, thin and stemmed, its shape designed to serve the wine rather than distract from it. A tulip-shaped bowl with a broad surface and a narrower rim allows the wine to breathe while keeping its aromas where they belong. There are a handful of makers – Zalto and Richard Brendon among them – and a few exceptional designs, such as the Conterno Sensory Glass, that consistently get this right. When decanting, I often use a slim carafe that sits happily in the fridge door. For special occasions, an old Georgian decanter does rather nicely.

WHERE WINE BEGINS

There's an inconvenient truth in the British wine trade: the average bottle sells for about £8, and at that price you're not really buying wine – you're buying tax, glass and the long journey it took to get here. The liquid? About 62 pence. At around £20, something shifts. Now a meaningful share of what you pay for is actually grown, not assembled. At a good independent merchant, the average bottle sits just under £17 – not a mark-up, but a sign of where that shift begins. So when a book plants its flag between £20 and £35, that isn't extravagance. It's where wine stops outperforming its price and begins to express its place.

●○○○○

£10–£20

Better than it should be

●●○○○

£21–£35

Where some of the smartest buying happens

Left Shrine to the Vine, Broadway Market, London

●●●○○

£36–£55

Wines that hold the dinner table

●●●●○

£56–£100

For serious eating

●●●●●

£100+

Wines that define the landscape

GLOSSARY

ACIDITY .... The essential backbone of a wine – lifting flavour, defining shape and keeping it fresh.

APPELLATION .... A legally defined wine-growing area whose name guarantees origin and often dictates grape varieties and practices.

ARTISANAL .... A term suggesting small-scale, hands-on production, with no fixed legal or technical definition.

BARRIQUE .... A small oak barrel, typically around 225 litres, used for fermenting or ageing wine and imparting more pronounced oak influence than larger casks.

BIODYNAMIC VITICULTURE ... A form of organic farming that treats the vineyard as a self-sustaining organism, guided by natural rhythms and informed by the ideas of Rudolf Steiner.

BLANC DE BLANCS .... A white sparkling wine made only from white grapes, most commonly Chardonnay.

BLANC DE NOIRS .... A white sparkling wine made from black grapes – typically Pinot Noir or Pinot Meunier – vinified without skin contact.

BOTTI .... Large Italian wooden casks used for ageing wine, typically imparting less oak flavour than small barrels.

CRU .... A French term meaning growth or vineyard; its specific significance – Cru Classé, Premier Cru, Grand Cru – is defined by regional classification systems and varies by region.

CUVÉE .... A specific batch or blend of wine, often selected or assembled for a particular bottling.

DOSAGE .... In sparkling wine, the small addition of sugar and wine added at bottling after disgorgement, used to adjust balance.

ÉLEVAGE .... The period and methods by which a wine is raised after fermentation, encompassing its ageing, handling and preparation for bottling.

FIELD BLEND .... A wine made from different grape varieties grown together in the same vineyard and harvested and fermented together.

FIRST GROWTH .... The highest rank in the 1855 Bordeaux classification, originally awarded to four châteaux and later extended to Château Mouton Rothschild in 1973.

FOUDRE .... A large wooden cask used for fermenting or ageing wine, imparting less overt oak influence than small barrels.

GRANDE MARQUE .... A term for the large, established Champagne houses, known chiefly for blended wines drawn from many vineyards, though some also bottle site-specific cuvées.

GROSSES GEWÄCHS (GG) ...... A designation of Germany's VDP for dry wines from a producer's top vineyard sites, made to strict standards and intended as the highest expression of place.

LEES .... The sediment of spent yeast cells and other solids left after fermentation, which may be left in contact with the wine to add texture, flavour and stability.

LIEU-DIT .... A named parcel of land, often a specific vineyard site, recognised locally long before formal appellations existed.

MALOLACTIC FERMENTATION A natural bacterial process that softens a wine by changing sharp, apple-like acidity into gentler, milkier acidity, giving the wine a rounder, smoother texture.

MINERALITY .... The stony impression in a wine – salt, struck match, wet rock rather than fruit – lending it precision and tension. An impressionistic shorthand rather than a scientific definition.

NATURAL WINE .... A loosely defined term for wines made with minimal intervention in vineyard and cellar, using native yeasts and little or no added sulphur, in pursuit of transparency of place and process.

NÉGOCIANT .... A wine merchant who buys grapes or finished wine and bottles it under their own name, historically central to regions such as Burgundy and the Rhône.

NOBLE ROT .... A beneficial infection of grapes by *Botrytis cinerea* that, under the right conditions, concentrates sugars and flavours to produce sweet wines of richness, balance and longevity.

NV (NON-VINTAGE) .... A designation for wines blended from multiple harvest years rather than a single vintage.

OLD VINES (*VIEILLES VIGNES*) An unregulated term indicating vines of advanced age, often associated with lower yields and greater concentration, but without a fixed legal meaning.

OXIDATIVE .... A conscious embrace of air in the cellar, favouring texture and resonance over freshness, with notes of walnut, apple skin, hay and spice. Not a flaw but a choice.

OXIDISED .... A wine spoiled by undue exposure to air, in which freshness, detail and vitality have been lost. Unlike oxidative winemaking, oxidation here is not expressive but destructive.

PAGO .... A distinct vineyard territory in Spain, defined by its soils, exposure and air. The character it lends its wines.

PHYLLOXERA................ A vine-destroying louse that devastated European vineyards in the 19th century and led to the grafting of *Vitis vinifera* onto resistant American rootstocks.

PREMATURE OXIDATION...... The untimely oxidation of a white wine, causing it to lose freshness and vitality well before its expected maturity. Often marked by browned colour, bruised fruit, stale aromas and a clipped finish.

REDUCTION .... A condition in which a wine, having had little contact with air, shows slightly sulphurous notes – struck match or flint – that often blow off with air, adding complexity in small amounts but a fault when dominant.

RESERVE/RISERVA/RÉSERVE .. Terms used in various countries to indicate wines subject to additional ageing requirements, whose precise meaning and legal weight vary by place and do not in themselves guarantee quality.

SAVOURY.................... A quality in wine that favours earth, herbs and umami over fruit, giving depth, complexity and an appetite-awakening character.

SOLERA..................... A system of fractional ageing and blending, chiefly used in Sherry, in which wines of different ages are continually refreshed to ensure continuity of style rather than expression of a single year.

SOUS-VOILE .... A Jura term for wines aged beneath a veil of yeast, lending nutty, saline, Sherry-like notes through slow biological ageing.

STRUCTURE .... The underlying framework of acidity, tannin, alcohol and extract that gives a wine shape, balance and the ability to develop over time.

SULPHUR .... An ancient safeguard against oxidation and spoilage, indispensable in many cellars and best when it leaves no fingerprint on the wine.

TANNINS .... Natural compounds from grape skins, seeds and sometimes stems or wood that give wine its drying, grippy texture and contribute to structure and ageing potential.

TERROIR.................... The French notion of a vineyard's total natural environment, expressed in wines with a distinctive sense of place.

TRADITIONAL METHOD....... The classic technique of making sparkling wine by a second fermentation in bottle, once called *méthode Champenoise*.

VIGNERON .... A winegrower who farms his or her own vines and makes wine from them, privileging agriculture, place and restraint over industrial production.

VILLAGE WINE............... In Burgundy, a wine made from vineyards entitled to a village appellation, such as Chambolle-Musigny.

VINTAGE..................... The year in which a wine's grapes were harvested, reflecting the particular conditions of that growing season.

VOLATILE ACIDITY .... The presence of sharp, evaporative acidity in a wine, perceptible as vinegar or nail-polish aromas when excessive, but lending lift and complexity in small amounts.

WHOLE BUNCH .... A winemaking approach in which intact grape clusters, including stems, are fermented rather than being destemmed.

INDEX

ABOUT THE AUTHOR

Dan Keeling is a London-based writer, restaurateur and wine merchant. He is the editor and co-founder of *Noble Rot* magazine and co-owner of three eponymous London restaurants, whose wine lists have won 'Wine List of the Year' at both the World Restaurant Awards and the National Restaurant Awards. With Mark Andrew, he runs Keeling Andrew, a wine import company working with some of the world's most compelling growers, alongside the Shrine to the Vine wine shops. His books include *Who's Afraid of Romanée-Conti?* (2024) and *Noble Rot: Wine from Another Galaxy*, which won the Guild of Food Writers' Drinks Book Award in 2021. His writing has appeared in *FT Weekend* and *El País*. Before wine, he worked in music, signing Coldplay and Lily Allen at Parlophone Records.

THANKS

They say you should write a book with someone in mind. I did. In fact, I had two: my dear friends Alex Bond and Mike Greek. Some time in the summer of 2025, when the title *Pick Your Bottles* first came into my head, I knew immediately who I was talking to. This book is for them – and for anyone like them – the curious, the enthusiastic, and those who want to drink better, on their own terms. I owe them thanks not only for their early encouragement, but also for the conversations and feedback that helped shape the book it became.

Much of what's here has been tried and tested on the restaurant floor, not behind a desk. In narrowing down the wines, I turned to the front-of-house team at Noble Rot to remind myself of what has endured: what *they* poured, what *they* loved, and what *they* reached for after service. Their answers came from genuine passion and a commitment to a métier that rewards care, curiosity and generosity. My thanks go to Alex Balgarnie, Ana Rey, Ben Thomas, Bronte Agostino, Chad Hamilton, Chloe Watt, Declan Foster, Elise Penney, Ellie Burt, Emma Swift, Evan Soloman, George Ball, Georgie McNamara, Grace Laughlin, Guy Whitelam, Jack Pepper, Jacob Desai Proud, Johnny Murphy, Jonah Calkin, Kat Mayhew, Kate Fyans, Kitty Cotton, Liv Kessler, Mally Capstick, Megan O'Rahilly, Ollie McSwiney, Ryan Goodale, Ryan Mostert, Terri Seeber, Terry Kandylis, Theo Millar, and Tom Greenhaigh.

Lastly, I am deeply grateful for the support of my longtime friend and collaborator Mark Andrew – with whom I've drunk more exceptional bottles than anyone else and built three companies along the way; Sarah Lavelle, Laura Willis, Katherine Case, Joel Rickett, and everyone at Quadrille; Cristina Paricio and the team at Cinco Tintas; Tom Pollard and Steve Fenn at Significant; Matt Willey; Ben McMahon; John Broadley; Nick Funnell; Luke Bird; Lesley Levene; Andrew Lewis; Tanya Layzell-Payne, Alice Grier, Lauren Fonda, and all at Becca; Robert Weiss; Fred Kaplin; Stephen Browett; Marina O'Loughlin; John Niven; and above all, my wife and best friend, Naomi Keeling. Every bottle in this book has tasted better with her.

Drink with pleasure. Drink with curiosity. Above all, keep drinking.

Quadrille, Penguin Random House UK,
One Embassy Gardens, 8 Viaduct Gardens,
London SW11 7BW

Quadrille Publishing Limited is part of the Penguin Random House group of companies whose addresses can be found at global.penguinrandomhouse.com

Penguin Random House UK

Published by Quadrille in 2026

www.penguin.co.uk

A CIP catalogue record for this book is available from the British Library

ISBN 9781807120313
10 9 8 7 6 5 4 3 2 1

Managing Director, Publishing: Sarah Lavelle
Copy Editor: Nick Funnell
Proofreaders: Lesley Levene and Lucy Kingett
Indexer: Helen Snaith
Art Direction: Dan Keeling
Text Design: Tom Pollard and Steve Fenn, Significant
Cover Design: Luke Bird
Head of Design: Katherine Case
Head of Production: Stephen Lang
Production Controller/Production Manager: Martina Georgieva

Colour reproduction by F1 Colour Ltd

Printed in China by C&C Offset Printing Co., Ltd.

The authorised representative in the EEA is Penguin Random House Ireland, Morrison Chambers, 32 Nassau Street, Dublin D02 YH68.

FSC www.fsc.org MIX Paper FSC® C018179

Penguin Random House is committed to a sustainable future for our business, our readers and our planet. This book is made from Forest Stewardship Council® certified paper.